THEATER
IN THE
AMERICAS

A Series from
Southern
Illinois
University
Press
ROBERT A.
SCHANKE
Series Editor

Other Books in the Theater in the Americas Series

The Theatre of Sabina Berman: The Agony of Ecstasy *and Other Plays*
Translated by Adam Versényi
With an Essay by Jacqueline E. Bixler

Composing Ourselves: The Little Theatre Movement and the American Audience
Dorothy Chansky

Women in Turmoil: Six Plays by Mercedes de Acosta
Edited and with an Introduction by Robert A. Schanke

Staging America: Cornerstone and Community-Based Theater
Sonja Kuftinec

Stage, Page, Scandals, and Vandals: William E. Burton and Nineteenth-Century American Theatre
David L. Rinear

"That Furious Lesbian": The Story of Mercedes de Acosta
Robert A. Schanke

Caffe Cino: The Birthplace of Off-Off-Broadway
Wendell C. Stone

Teaching Performance Studies
Edited by Nathan Stucky and Cynthia Wimmer
With a Foreword by Richard Schechner

OUR LAND IS MADE OF COURAGE AND GLORY

OUR LAND
IS MADE
OF COURAGE
AND GLORY

NATIONALIST PERFORMANCE OF
NICARAGUA AND GUATEMALA

E. J. Westlake

Southern Illinois University Press / Carbondale

Printed in the United States of America
08 07 06 05 4 3 2 1

Library of Congress Cataloging-in-Publication Data
    Westlake, E. J., 1965–
    Our land is made of courage and glory : nationalist
performance of Nicaragua and Guatemala / E. J. Westlake
        p. cm. — (Theater in the Americas)
    Includes bibliographical references and index.
    1. Nicaraguan drama—20th century—History and
criticism. 2. Guatemalan drama—20th century—History
and criticism. 3. Nationalism in literature. 4. Nationalism
and literature—Nicaragua. 5. Nationalism and literature—
Guatemala. I. Title. II. Series.
    PQ7513.W47 2005
    862'.609358—dc22   2004023655
    ISBN 0-8093-2625-6 (cloth : alk. paper)

Printed on recycled paper. ♻

The paper used in this publication meets the minimum
requirements of American National Standard for Information Sciences—Permanence of Paper for Printed Library
Materials, ANSI Z39.48-1992. ∞

Through the fatal pages of history,
our land is made of courage and glory,
our land is made for Humanity.

People vibrant, strong, passionate, proud;
people aware of being alive,
and so, bringing their energies together in a powerful
beam, to the Motherland they courageously reveal
that they can bravely wield the sword of war
in the right hand or the olive branch of peace.

When Dante took science to the Sorbonne
and his wonderful Florentine heart,
I believe he expressed the soul of Florence,
and his city was in the divine book.

If the Motherland is small, one dreams it great.
My illusions, and my desires, and my
hopes tell me there is no small Motherland.

—Rubén Darío, "The Return"

Contents

Contents

Illustrations

Acknowledgments

I would like to thank my series editor, Bob Schanke. He saw the potential in this book and was patient and understanding as the work progressed. I would also like to thank the staff at Southern Illinois University Press, particularly Karl Kageff, Kristine Priddy, Carol Burns, Barb Martin, Wayne Larsen, Jane Carlson, and Katherine Faydash.

I would like to acknowledge the Wisconsin Coordinating Council on Nicaragua (WCCN), Carrie Hirsch, and Julie Andersen. The WCCN facilitated bringing Ocho de Marzo to the United States and organized one of my trips to Nicaragua during my research. I would like to thank my Nicaraguan friends Rubén Reyes and Monserrat Fernández for all of their help tracking down people and materials and for making my last trip to Nicaragua so fruitful. They are wonderful scholars and good people, and they have opened my eyes to many things.

The University of Michigan School of Music and Auburn University College of Liberal Arts both provided funding for research travel. My theatre studies colleagues at the University of Michigan—Leigh Woods; Glenda Dickerson; Mbala Nkanga; and Oyamo; my department chair, Erik Fredriksen; and the supportive theatre department staff, Becky Seauvageau and Bonnie Kerschbaum— have all made it possible for me to do my research and complete this project.

I would like to thank my colleague and friend Tamara Underiner for her continued support through the years. Tamara saw this project at the beginning and gave me much-needed feedback.

For introducing me to the realm of ideas about nationalism, race, historicism, and memorialization, I want to thank James Moy, Sally Banes, Mary Karen Dahl, Jill Dolan, Jack Kugelmass, Luis Madureira, Leigh Payne, and Shu-chin Wu.

I want to thank my wonderful partner, Claudia Wier, for her encouragement, understanding, and friendship through the years, and my thoughtful and beautiful stepson, Travis, for being so patient with me while I was working at home. I am grateful to all the members of my family, immediate and extended, who have looked after me and given me the foundation from which to venture out into the world.

I also want to thank my mother, Joy, and my father, Curtis. I hope to honor their memory with this text. Together they inspired my desire to learn, my love for literature, and my hope for social justice.

OUR LAND IS MADE OF COURAGE AND GLORY

Introduction
Moving Statues

The statue of Anastasio Somoza, which stood in the plaza of the Palacio Nacional, was pulled down and broken during the fighting at the end of Nicaragua's 1979 Sandinista Revolution. All that remained of the statue was the back end of the horse on which Somoza was mounted. After the fighting ended, the Sandinistas left the monument where it lay. They found that the remaining fragment made a fitting monument to the deposed dictator, a horse's ass.

The image of the surviving statue fragment made its way into one of the most famous of the Sandinista murals painted after the Revolution. *Our Land Is Made of Courage and Glory,* a mural in León named for a line in a poem by the national poet Rubén Darío, represents all of Nicaraguan history, beginning with pre-Columbian petroglyphs and ending with two children running from the desert to Lake Managua with the volcano Momotombo in the background. In between are the traces of conquistadores; blood-drenched flags; a book and spectacles belonging to Carlos Fonseca; the last letter of Rigoberto López Pérez, the man who assassinated Anastasio Somoza; and the "Somoza" bricks, used as barricades by the revolutionaries, lying next to the horse's rear. Over the past decade, the mural, still standing, has been in continual danger of being completely erased.

In late 1990 the democratically elected president of Nicaragua, Violeta Chamorro, began a program of systematically painting over many of the murals that were commissioned after the popular revolution of 1979. Her election in 1990 was supposed to signal the end of internal struggle in Nicaragua between supporters of the Sandinistas and a hodgepodge of opposition parties that received strong backing from the United States. Chamorro's coalition, the Unión Nacional Opositora (National

1

Opposition Union, or UNO), was elected by a very narrow margin, giving the Sandinistas in the parliamentary government a wide range of continuing control. Still, whatever could be erased of the revolutionary culture was indeed erased.

The monument to Somoza has undergone a series of remarkable transformations as power has shifted in Nicaragua and as its history is redefined. The twists and turns in this struggle for meaning expose a complex set of relationships among those who seek to define what a Nicaraguan nation must be. From the Somoza "dynasty," in which Anastasio's son saw fit to erect a statue of his father in the main square as a sign of Somoza regime legitimacy, to the Sandinista redeployment of the sign as both the history of the dictatorship and of the popular feeling toward the dictator, to Chamorro's threats to erase the sign, the nation emerges and reemerges as a string of performances that define Nicaragua by the rejection and continuation of what has gone before. The "fact" of the statue is continuous, but the deployment of the sign of the statue has changed with each bend in the political landscape.

Every rupture in a national history, such as a revolution, brings a flurry of new cultural activity. Out of the turmoil of protests and political rallies, new flags are flown, new anthems created. The citizenry are called upon to participate and thereby legitimate the new national culture. Traditions are invoked or invented. In Nicaragua, for example, a Ministry of Culture was created with the revolutionary poet Ernesto Cardinal as its minister. Poetry was written in classrooms as part of the new literacy drive, and Nicaraguans were reminded that they are naturally poets and have a poetic tradition as long as the history of the nation itself.

Similarly, a cry for a state theatre often accompanies new national formation. In Nicaragua and Guatemala, dramatists and nationalists alike felt strongly that a new national culture included rediscovering forgotten theatrical traditions. The dramatic literature that grew out of these efforts attempted to capture a particular national essence, one that, because of the public nature of the dramatic form, would be witnessed and confirmed by the citizens in the audience.

Both the treatment of the material within the drama and the establishment of the national theatre as an institution serve a joint purpose. As with the statue of Somoza, what can be called "facts," the real geographical land of the nation and the actual events that make up historical accounts, do exist. How the facts are configured by the writer and the audience of national drama shifts with each historical rupture. Through national drama, the playwrights attempt to nail down for each moment the nature of the nation.

The chapters that follow look critically at Central American plays as nationalist performance. They analyze the ways the nation is configured and revised through the presentation of metaphors in nationalist play texts, in this case, the play texts of Guatemala and Nicaragua. The two countries began with a shared history as part of a larger colonial territory. Both have dealt with internal strife, fed in part by economic imperialism and military intervention by the United States. More important, both nations have had periods of national redefinition that have generated a remarkable body of nationalist literature.

Within these nationalist movements, playwrights created texts that reveal the ways national identity is performed, legitimated, and deployed. The texts offer for the national audience images of who belongs within the nation, who the outsiders are, the common values held by the citizens, and the events that led to the liberation of the nation. These plays offer a cross section of images that, when performed, construct the nation, the national history, and a sense of national continuity.

The following chapters provide a broad analysis of these images within the drama of Guatemala and Nicaragua, beginning with the cultural and historical background necessary for comprehending the national drama of these two countries. In the past, scholars have presented Latin American drama outside of its historical and political context, which has led to a warping of the meaning of the text. As Juan Villegas noted in 1989: "Previously, hegemonic critical discourse has included the marginal Latin American works only when they can be interpreted as 'universal.'"[1] Western scholars have continually privileged the aesthetic of European surrealism, or even the frame of Jungian psychoanalysis,[2] when examining the Mayan-influenced work of Miguel Ángel Asturias, and have read the indigenous Mayan text of the *Rabinal Achí* through the model of Greek tragedy or Noh theatre. Hugo Carrillo (1928–1994) rejected such warping when his highly visible debate with Joseph Papp led him to withdraw his adaptation of Asturias's novel *El Señor Presidente* from the New York Latin American Festival in 1987.[3] Villegas suggests that scholars take a more historiographic approach and consider time, location, and audience. This book joins a growing body of Latin American theatre scholarship that reads the literature through its political and historical context.

The scholarship of nationalism and nationalist culture frames this analysis of performance and dramatic literature. Over the past two decades, the body of writing on nationalism and culture has grown and is most effectively manifest in the anthology edited by Homi K. Bhabha, *Nation and Narration. Nationalism, Colonialism, and Literature,* the collaborative work of Terrence Eagleton, Fredric Jameson, and Edward Said, analyzes nationalism and culture in Ireland. Doris Sommer writes about the Latin American romance novel and nationalism in *Foundational Fictions.* One of the first texts to focus on nationalism and theatre was the seminal work by Loren Kruger, *The National Stage,* which focuses exclusively on developed nations. Since then, the body of work on nationalism and theatre in postcolonial nations has virtually exploded, covering areas from Australia, as in Helen Gilbert's *Sightlines,* to the thorny issues of bilingual national identities in *Performing Identities on the Stages of Quebec* by Jill Mac Dougall. Probably the three most effective texts to wrestle with these concepts in Latin America are Adam Versényi's *Theatre in Latin America*, Diana Taylor's *Disappearing Acts,* and Randy Martin's *Socialist Ensembles.* This work joins these authors in attempting to situate theatre practice within the shifting political matrices that make up nationalist and postcolonial discourse.

As these previously mentioned writers demonstrate, configuring the nation is troubled enough in first-world, or colonizing and imperialist, nations. In *Imagined Communities,* Benedict Anderson points to the contradiction between the very recent emergence of the nation as a concept at all and the fact that the power of the concept lay in the belief in the nation's antiquity.[4] How, then, does one address the issue of nationhood in a more contested situation, the developing countries of the so-called third world? Does nation exist as geography? As a set of force relations or institutions? Does it only exist in the minds of those who feel they belong? Does the definition originate from outside; is it an imposition of a colonizing power onto colonized land? The answer to this question lies within the complex and shifting articulations of these ideas. The "facts" of the nation's history provide a starting point for addressing these questions.

Several forces shape the unique quality of nationalism in Latin America: regionalism, imperialism, Catholicism, and popular culture. Latin American nations grew out of criollo (American-born Europeans) resistance against what they considered unfair treatment from the Iberian governments. The similar colonization practices of a common colonial government and the solidarity of the Latin American nations in fighting for independence lends a kind of regionalism not found on most continents. But nationalism is strong enough to imprint decisive borders, despite some attempts to make larger federations out of some of the more cohesive regions; Central America is a case in point. Several of the nationalist plays written in Central America have strong regionalist ideas as well. For instance, Manuel José Arce (1933–1985), a Guatemalan playwright, used the story of the history of Nicaragua in *¡Viva Sandino! (Sandino Lives!)* to express his hopes for Guatemala.

Imperialism also shapes nationalist movements in this region. Since colonial times, imperialist forces such as the United States have played a large role in the formation of nationalist movements in Latin America, especially in Central America. The United States has historically intervened often and directly in the affairs of its closest neighbors. Countries that are the targets of economic and military domination must struggle to maintain their sense of national identity, their feeling of nationhood. These countries perform the nation both as defined by and as defined against those forces, creating what Isaac Cohen refers to as a "defensive nationalism."[5] In Central America and the Caribbean, where the pressure from the United States is particularly intense, dramatists and activists alike have had little opportunity to discover what the nation might look like free from the invasive efforts of the United States.

Catholicism also forms an important part of Latin American culture throughout history. The church had an active role in the colonization process of the Latin American countries, and it continues to hold much power in the shaping of Latin American society and politics. The liberal parties in many countries, such as those in Nicaragua, made it part of their platform to limit the power of the church in favor of a more civil government. During the 1960s, after Vatican II, a debate unfolded within the church that drew the lines between the conservative church and the liberation theologists who often took up the fight against imperialism. This influence runs through some, but not all, of the plays discussed here. Although Pablo Antonio Cuadra (1912–2002) believed in a Christian solution to the plight of a family caught up in the partisan warfare of Nicaragua, other Marxist-leaning writers, such as Manuel Galich (1913–1983) and Alan Bolt (c. 1951–), rejected the church and Christianity. They sought socialist solutions to the problem of nationalism being under the pressure of imperialism. Asturias and other Guatemalans even embraced the pre-Christian Mayan culture as more truly American than the Catholic church.

Although mass media grew in popularity in the latter part of the twentieth century, it seems less effective in shaping a national consciousness than does the tradition-forming national drama. The mass media of

Central America is often regional rather than local, and television programs are syndicated from Argentina, Brazil, and Honduras. Also, the act of producing and attending national theatre makes citizens active participants in nation building. The self-identification of each Nicaraguan as a poet, or the tradition of high drama in Guatemala, puts the act of the formation of the national character at a micro level of production. This is unlike the consumption of mass media, during which images are projected onto passive observers.

The most compelling reason to deal exclusively with staged culture rather than mass media relates to current theory on nationalism, which casts the idea of the nation as a construct. In my view, nations are neither real nor imagined but are performed. The citizens of the nation continually reflect, alter, and construct the nation through such cultural products as anthems, parades, protests, newspapers, and literature. Only through this performance does the nation become "real" in the imaginations of the citizens/audience members as they acknowledge and ratify the images of the nation through their rehearsal and repetition. It is for this reason that I believe theatre and the dramatic literature meant for performance in the theatre offer an ideal location for examining this articulation in action.

A nationalist play offers insights into the ways the nation is realized for and by the citizen/audience member in three significant ways. First, the play defines the dimensions of the nation in terms of creating a national metaphor, using a national language, and creating a "people." Second, the play creates a sense of national history that is shared by the citizens/audience members. Third, the play creates a sense of national continuity, through both the performance of the national history and the projection of the current values commonly held by the citizens/audience members back into an earlier time period.

The parts that follow focus on certain dramatists and their plays as case studies of nationalist ideas in practice in national drama. Part one covers a brief history of the nationalist theatre in Guatemala and Nicaragua. It also sets the basic theoretical frame for discussing nationalism and nationalist performance. Part two covers two important Guatemalan dramatists and their most important dramatic works. Chapter 4 examines the work of Manuel Galich, a prolific Guatemalan playwright who began his career writing *costumbres*, or domestic comedies, and eventually became one of the most important Guatemalan playwrights of the twentieth century. Galich's nationalist plays include a trilogy that follows the Natas family through the dictatorship, the revolution, and the coup that ended Guatemala's democratic government. *El tren amarillo* (*The Yellow Train*) (1954), perhaps his most interesting play, gives us a snapshot of the ideal Guatemalan citizen during the revolutionary regime of 1944–54. Through the characters of the drama, Galich draws a boundary around those considered citizens of the country and those considered outsiders. However, on closer examination, the text reveals that the boundary is a shifting and unstable one and is only newly reconstructed in the revolutionary culture. Galich also wrote plays incorporating Mayan mythology, including a children's play about Gukup-Cakix, the giant who is outwitted and destroyed by the first humans in the great Mayan mythology text, the Popul Vuh.

Chapter 5 covers the work of Miguel Ángel Asturias (1899–1974), a Nobel Prize laureate and an influential novelist in Guatemala. Asturias believed in reviving Mayan culture and employing Mayan imagery and stories in his drama. *Soluna* (literally, *Sunmoon*) (1955) is a case in point, a drama that uses a Mayan dance of a war between the sun and moon to demonstrate the warring feelings of the main character. Asturias also wrote *Audencia de los confines* (*Tribunal on the Frontier*) (1957), a play that uses the story of Bartolomé de las Casas and the New Laws, a decree championed by Las Casas that freed indigenous people from slavery, to make a point about the plight of the modern Mayan people.

The chapters of part two provide an examination of the ways nationalist drama creates a "people." The drama examined in this part uses metaphor to draw specific national boundaries and to define which people are contained within the national borders compared with those people who are not. National theatre also creates a national "race." In Guatemala and Nicaragua this takes the form of the introduction of the mestizo character into the national drama. In the case of Galich's *El tren amarillo,* the drama includes characters from a diverse range of ethnic backgrounds, establishing a racial brotherhood and replacing the older notion that *Guatemalan* meant the Guatemalan criollo: those born in Guatemala but who are of European descent. A resurgence of interest in Mayan culture in Guatemala produced several dramas that included indigenous characters and stories.

Several of the plays include characters that are considered undesirable foreigners, in sharp contrast to the ideal citizen. Because of the continuous struggle with the United States, several Yankee characters march in and out of these texts; their heinous actions incite courageous and patriotic reactions from the ideal indigenous citizens within each story. Yankees are not the only contrasting literary trope used in the plays; Galich's Chinese storeowner provides an interesting contrast to the ideal Guatemalan in *El tren amarillo*.

Part three is dedicated to an examination of the work of Nicaraguan dramatists. The history of partisan warfare and the struggle against foreign economic domination that led up to the Sandinista Revolution produced drama that reconfigured the national history. Part three will focus on the construction of history as part of the construction of national identity.

Chapter 7 is an analysis of the work of Alan Bolt, the director of the Nixtayolero theatre troupe. Bolt's play, *Banana Republic* (1982), offers a linear view of Nicaraguan history through the eyes of someone who supports the idea of a progressive revolution. For Bolt, Nicaraguan history follows a logical progression, in the Marxist sense, to a worker-led government. Chapter 7 will examine *Banana Republic* and the development of Bolt's company as yet another call to reviving an invented tradition.

Chapter 8 compares Bolt with the earlier work of Pablo Antonio Cuadra, a founding member of Vanguardia, the Nicaraguan Vanguard movement. This movement began as part of a conservative project by artists and intellectuals who allied themselves with fascist ideology and the repressive Somoza regime. Its program of recovering language and performance forms that were distinctly Nicaraguan led an overall call to establish theatre groups all over the country. This was the impetus behind Cuadra's play *Por los caminos van los campesinos* (*Down the Road the Peasants Go*) (1937), a play that incorporated supposedly traditional street performance techniques. Unlike Bolt's linear construction of history, Cuadra's ideal of the revolutionary impulse as parricidal belies the Vanguardia's desire to return to tradition, a tradition that is largely constructed.

By contrast, Rolando Steiner's (1932–) *La noche de Wiwilí* (*The Night of Wiwilí*) (1982) recalls the night Sandino was murdered by Somoza's men, right after he had honored a treaty that called for his army to turn in their weapons. Steiner wrote the play from an official account, and he configures the event as a logical precursor to the Sandinista Revolution of 1979. The play offers a glimpse of the process by which history is constructed and reconstructed as it passes from lived memory into preserved "official" memory. Chapter 9 takes up this critical examination of memory and history.

Part three examines the ways history is performed in national drama.

David Lowenthal, in *The Past Is a Foreign Country,* states that people use the past to render the present familiar, to reaffirm and validate present attitudes by demonstrating their resemblance to former ones, and to provide a historical figure with which the present-day citizen can identify (such as Augusto Sandino).[6] National historical drama emerges out of a desire to renegotiate the past with the present, to show "the people" as a product of a long and continuing journey from the past into an eternal future.

The continuity sought through this process is also the subject of part three. The national dramatist reconfigures the trauma of the historical rupture of revolution as the emergence of something true and continuous, something suppressed by colonial or imperialist forces. The ambivalence of this fragmentation/continuity drives each nationalist performance with even more earnestness and desperation, particularly when the threat of the invading force's return looms always on the horizon.

Previously, Latin American scholars have generally ignored Central American drama because of the chauvinism of wealthier and "whiter" countries toward poorer mestizo nations. It is only in the last half of the twentieth century that Latin American drama emerged as a field of study in the United States at all; previously, Spain was the only Spanish-speaking country deemed worthy of attention by European American scholars. Similarly, European-derived people of Argentina, Chile, Cuba, Puerto Rico, and Mexico garnered most of the attention for European-influenced theatre performances. Accordingly, nations that have a national culture defined in opposition to this influence have rarely been studied in English. It is precisely this opposition, however, that makes these plays so compelling as nationalist drama.

In this book, I attempt to pin down the idea of the nation through its performance in national drama, with the acknowledgment that the idea of nation and the attempt to make it a coherent construct ultimately fails. Not only does it fail because of the instability of its constructedness, but also it fails in Central America because of the instability of national sovereignty. The imperialist impulses of the United States chip away at any political, and thereby cultural, autonomy that Central American nations have. I was in Nicaragua in 1989, shortly before the national elections, and I witnessed later, from home, how effectively the United States created an electoral outcome that again reshaped the direction of the Nicaraguan nation. Through intimidation by contra troops and funding an opposition party, the United States ensured the defeat of the Sandinistas, the revolutionary party. The victory of Violeta Chamorro marked a reversal of the signs deployed as part of the revolutionary culture.

Also, the national, usually "high," drama represents the clashing ideas of the elite ruling classes.[7] As I point out in subsequent chapters, the cultural products that are canonized emerge out of clashes among ruling parties vying for cultural hegemony. With a few valuable exceptions, the people, for the benefit of whom nationalist dramas are written, seldom produce works that are memorialized into the national canon. This involves the issue of gender as well, in that men write most of the high drama and make a majority of the decisions involving projects of national theatre. In an attempt to address this issue in Nicaragua, the Sandinista program decentralized culture in the 1980s and put it into the hands of small groups for very specific purposes.

Finally, my position as a white scholar from an imperialist country shapes the way I read these plays. I have even thought that it is perhaps colonizing to work through these texts from a position where I am looking through *lentes norteamericanos*—or North American glasses—as Alan Bolt has said.[8] That is a thought I have not, and cannot, negotiate with my work. My position as "institutionally privileged"[9] explains, perhaps, my own bias in wanting to quickly point out that nations are a construct. I join the chorus of those in the first world who luxuriously call the idea of "nation" into question while third-world nationalists struggle to find their voice.

Even as these threads of the concept of nation threaten to unravel, the insistence of the national drama in the realness of the nation provides plenty to examine. Each scene written by the nationalist dramatist presents the audience with a view of itself: a people with a history and a people with a future.

PART ONE
NATIONALISM AND LATIN AMERICAN DRAMA

1 HISTORICAL BACKGROUND

The coherent nation, and therefore the national theatre, evolved in Guatemala and Nicaragua despite internal obstacles and the restriction of U.S. imperialism. Although the Latin American countries fought for independence from Spain in the early nineteenth century, certain social forces, such as strong regionalism and a feudal, agrarian social system, worked against the formation of coherent national identities. The shift toward modernization in the twentieth century and the weakening of the feudal structure by U.S. intervention cleared the way for a stronger sense of national identity. However, both Guatemala and Nicaragua have distinct histories that shape the distinct character of the national culture.

Indigenous Ritual and Dance Drama

A discussion of the national theatre of Guatemala and Nicaragua must begin with a discussion of what we know, or what we think we know, of the indigenous culture and performance forms. Although the modern nation is a construct of the European colonizer, the Central American nations are products of the hybridization of the indigenous with other world cultures. Initially three cultures blended in the early years of colonization (European, African, and indigenous), and there are even more forces to consider throughout history: later European immigrants, immigrants from Asia, and the persistent cultural hegemony of the United States. The demographic makeup of present-day Nicaragua and Guatemala testify to this diversity.

It is also important to acknowledge that the indigenous cultures of the different regions of Central America are quite distinct and have had unique roles in helping shape the modern national image. Guatemala's indigenous population is largely Mayan, and many Mayan communities are intact, identifying as Mayan and using Mayan languages and practicing Mayan customs. As a result, the mestizo (or in Guatemala *ladino*), the mixed indigenous and European, population in Guatemala is smaller than that of Nicaragua. Nicaragua was made up of several groups of people unrelated in language or culture. The group that settled along the narrow isthmus between Lake Nicaragua and the Pacific, on the islands in Lake Nicaragua, and on the northern shore of the lake are culturally and linguistically related to the Nahuas, the Aztec people of central Mexico. The tribal leader was named Niquirano, and the region was named for him. The group that the invading Aztecs displaced called themselves *mánkeme,* or "rulers." The word was later corrupted to *Mangues* by the Spanish. They were given the name *chololteca* (pronounced *chorotega*) by the Aztecs, or "the ones driven out."[1] Additionally, the East Coast communities of Nicaragua are made up of indigenous Miskito people and descendants of African slaves, whose hybrid cultures formed under the colonization of Great Britain. The presence of these two groups makes the character of eastern Nicaragua something altogether different from that of western and central Nicaragua.

The Mayan people, living in the Guatemalan highlands, have remained a coherent subculture within Guatemala, enabling much of Mayan language and culture to remain intact. Today, the indigenous people make up 45 percent of the population, the mestizo people 45 percent, and the white population approximately 5 percent.[2] In Nicaragua, however, the native population of Mangues and Nahuas were practically wiped out by the Spanish. Daniel Brinton notes in his study of the two tribes of 1883 that "scarcely any pure-blood remnants of either of these nations can be found, and both languages are practically extinct."[3] Presently, Nicaragua's population is 69 percent mestizo, 17 percent white, and only 5 percent indigenous.[4]

Dance, costumes, masks, and, in many cases, humor, are all elements of preconquest performance. Nikolai Grube notes that hieroglyphs depicting dancers with masks often appeared in texts inscribed during the Mayan Classical period, showing that dance was a central element of Mayan culture.[5] One Mayan dance drama, the *Rabinal Achí,* still survives and chronicles the struggle between the Quiché Mayans and the Rabinal Mayans. In a text that is indicative of the ritualistic nature of warfare, the Quiché warrior accepts his capture by the Rabinal warrior. Common foot soldiers were often enslaved by their captors. The Quiché warrior is the highest-ranking warrior of his people and will be sacrificed. He prepares to die the honorable death that is accorded someone of his rank. In the mid-nineteenth century, the French scholar Pierre Brasseur de Bourbourg translated the Mayan Quiché version of *Rabinal Achí* into French. George Raynaud at the Sorbonne also translated the text into French. It was translated into Spanish by Miguel Ángel Asturias and Luis Cardoza y Aragón from Raynaud's version in 1929–30. It was later translated into Spanish by Francisco Monterde, who used both Brasseur's and Raynaud's French versions as well as Brasseur's original Quiché text.

Dance played an important role in the indigenous cultures of Central America, and many of the dance performances and customs have survived. Daniel Brinton observed in 1883 that dance continued to serve a religious function in Nicaragua:

> Thus it is still a common custom, in case of sickness or impending danger, to make a vow that, in case of escape, the person will dance before the image of some saint on a certain day, at a certain place, usually at a festival.[6]

Before the image of the saint, the physical performance of the dance equals the spoken prayer or mantra in importance.

Many ethnographers have attempted to categorize the various types of preconquest performance, either by form or by function.[7] However, applying distinctions broadly across such different cultures proves difficult. It is also difficult to determine what is purely indigenous, what is syncretic, and how much these forms have changed over time.

The Catholic church attempted to destroy as much of the indigenous culture as possible. The Spanish destroyed Aztec and Mayan texts and banned rituals. However, they did not succeed in completely wiping away all traces of indigenous performance. Brinton notes that

> the old authors refer to [scenic performance] frequently, and the early missionaries, finding that they could not extinguish it, sought to turn it to good account by substituting for native plays, which were idolatrous or licentious, moral and instructive pieces. They encouraged the more intelligent natives and half-breeds to prepare such, and they were acted in connection with church festivals.[8]

The Catholic church saw fit to suppress any heathen rituals and performances, replacing them with the Christian drama brought from Spain. According to the writer Hugo Carrillo, in his article on the origins of Guatemalan theatre:

> [The priests] adapted the local dances, removing from them their pagan spirit, and introduced dramatic expressions brought from Spain and imposed them upon the indigenous for religious and political purposes. The catechizing

theatre was an effective way to enslave the conquered. Dances of Moors and Christians and of the Conquest appeared, where the Indians confront the Spaniards, are conquered, and then ask the victors for the Christian baptism.[9]

The agents of the church would even disguise Spanish drama with indigenous elements in an attempt to erase the indigenous culture.[10] Several scholars argue that the native people found ways to subvert colonial authority and church ideology.

Judith Weiss, Adam Versényi, and Max Harris all note the apparently contradictory semiotics of *La conquista de Jerusalén* (*The Conquest of Jerusalem*) (1543). The Nahuas of Tlaxcala performed the piece at the feast of Corpus Christi under the supervision of the Franciscans. In the performance, the Christians liberated Jerusalem from the Moors. However, in a layering of symbols, the Christians were dressed as the Viceroy Antonio de Mendoza, the new captain general of New Spain. The Moors were dressed like the former captain general and the conqueror of the Aztecs, Hernán Cortés. Versényi observes that, at the same time the Christians were defeating the Moors, there was an "Indian army defeating an army led by Cortés . . . , thus reversing the history of the Conquest."[11] Although no one can be sure of the motivation of the Tlaxcalans for writing the piece in this way, or of the Franciscans for allowing it, the performance shows one means of possible subversion in the reversals of signification.

Indigenous and mestizo peasants also created hybrid forms of performance, several of which were also subversive to colonial authority. Brinton supposes that *El Güegüence,* a Nicaraguan dance drama, emerged around the beginning of the seventeenth century. The piece uses both Nahuatl and Spanish, a combination that creates clever double meanings. In the play, Güegüence (a name that probably comes from the Nahuatl word *huehue,* or "old man") goes to see the governor. Initially, the governor means to get the old man's money, but Güegüence tricks the governor, by feigning misunderstanding and by twisting the meaning of what he says, into marrying his daughter to Güegüence's son. If *La conquista de Jerusalén* uses images to subvert colonial power, *El Güegüence* and its kind use language to achieve the same end.

As we look back at the precolonial and colonial cultures of Central America and attempt to read the signs left from the performances, we must acknowledge the difficulty in reading through the layers of history. Many of the indigenous and hybrid performance forms were recorded by agents of the church. Many others were collected by European anthropologists in the nineteenth century. Ideas of what these performances must mean have changed tremendously over the past five hundred years, but the threads of these practices filter through and influence the national culture of the twentieth century.

The Struggle for Independence from Spain

Central America was the site of frequent conflicts between the colonizers and the indigenous population, originally enslaved by the Spaniards. Bartolomé de las Casas, eventually the bishop of Chiapas, petitioned the Spanish crown to free the indigenous people. Eventually, Charles I agreed, and the indigenous people were officially freed from slavery under the New Laws of 1542. Often, the Spanish continued enslavement through unofficial means, but, in many instances, they replaced indigenous slaves with enslaved Africans.

Guatemala held a very important position in colonial Central America. The capital city (which moved more than once because of frequent devastation by earthquakes) became the captaincy general, or Audencia, of Central America in 1549. Policy for the region was made at the Audencia.

Although political power remained relatively centralized in colonial Guatemala, the government in Nicaragua was already beginning to factionalize in the sixteenth and seventeenth centuries. The government was originally seated in Granada, a town on the great Lake Nicaragua. A group was sent north in the early sixteenth century to found León, in order to secure the northern provinces from possible attacks from El Salvador and Honduras. While old landholding families held the power in the south, the shipbuilders, merchants, and small coffee growers became a formidable presence in the north.[12]

Throughout the eighteenth century, the British attempted to gain control of the Atlantic coast of Central America, but they withdrew from the Mosquito Coast and Bay Islands after the Treaty of Versailles in 1783 and the Convention of London in 1786. At the beginning of the nineteenth century, Spain was attempting to recover from the Napoleonic Wars. The Spanish raised taxes and censored the press in the colonies. Some of the repressive measures were lifted after Spain had a liberal revolution in 1820, but by then most of the Latin American nations, with the exception of Cuba, were in the full swing of independence movements.

This continent-wide movement did not necessarily arise out of a strong feeling of national identity, but out of the desire of the ruling families to have more power and to be free of the heavy taxes imposed by the crown.

The strong regionalism of the area grew out of the involuntary separation between the European-born and the criollos. Only European-born men could hold the highest posts of any colonial government, and the Spanish aristocracy held the distinct attitude that those born in the Americas were somehow inferior. The criollo class of each nation possessed enough nationalist sentiment such that each colonial region retained its original borders, more or less, after 1821. Out of this sentiment the early forms of nationalist literature developed. As Marina Pianca states:

> The new nations, that we call Latin America today, were born after an arduous liberating fight in order to face the task of working and making the future. Under these circumstances, the nation and literature were born together, and it is not surprising that literature was assigned the social project of inventing the future.[13]

The ruling elite began to imagine their new community. At the time, however, the caudillo system did not allow for the kind of social mobility that creates the conditions necessary for a full-fledged nationalist movement to exist.[14]

The Caudillo Period and Partisan Warfare

The Latin American colonies were made up of large plantations called *latifundios,* which were geared toward the production of large volumes of raw materials. Because of this, the landed elite who took up the struggle for independence were dispersed over vast territories. This made the consolidation of state power difficult:

> Spanish America ... faced the problem of decapitation of a legitimate structure of central authority (whatever its limits and weaknesses) represented by the crown in Spain, and the impossibility, given the size and geographic dispersion of territories, of creating even a weak central authority.[15]

This dispersion, coupled with the contrast between the urban elite of the national capitals and the landed, rural class, created a formula more prone to civil war than to nation building. The urban elite began to develop constitutional structures and a more dynamic economy. The rural landowners relied on patronage as a political structure and needed the stability of the status quo.

The rural power structure, or the patron-client relationship, was vertical rather than horizontal. Instead of a social structure built around an identification with a class, the patron-client relationship was based on identification with a feudal *patrón,* or landowner. The landowner relied upon a feudal system of control based on the *latifundio.* The *patrón's* family, a system of administrators, and then, finally, the peasants, worked in a system of mutual benefit whereby the peasant could count on the protection of the *patrón,* and the *patrón* could count on the loyalty of the peasant. Political agreements were made between powerful families. If the liberal government developing in the metropolis threatened the power of these families in any way, an army of peasants could be raised, and the caudillo, a general representing the rural interest, could take the urban government by force. The rural class formed the early conservative political parties and the more urban merchant class evolved into the early liberal parties.

The Central American countries of Guatemala, Honduras, El Salvador, Nicaragua, and Costa Rica tried to remain together as a federation after their independence in 1821. Leaders of the Central American nations made several accords and a federal constitution allowing for the election of a federation president from any of the five countries. But disagreement between the various heads of state over who should hold office caused the effort to fall apart by 1838. Several state leaders attempted to bring about a reunification either by negotiation or by force.

The *Costumbre*

The national theatre in Central America has, as its roots, the popular theatre of the beginning of the twentieth century. Dramatic writers had, until that point, imitated the works of European writers or had booked performers touring from Europe. Intellectuals believed in the superiority of the neoclassical model, and popular forms such as melodrama found commercial success. National drama begins as writers look for ways to transfer the unique characteristics of the nation to the stage. How much of the European culture to retain as an influence became a central issue for Central American dramatists. As Pianca states:

> [T]he future branches off in the minds of its creators and thus two contra-
> dictory visions took form for the manifestation of a Latin American destiny.
> Visions that, at this point in time, become ingrained in the collective imagi-
> nation that still marks the development of the continent. We are referring
> to the concepts present in the work of the Argentinean Domingo Faustino
> Sarmiento and the Cuban Jose Martí: one, eager to foment "progress" by
> applying models from Europe and the United States, the other, distrustful

of any form of colonialism, leading the task of constructing a free, dignified and integrated America, that he simply called "Our America." The Latin American theatre and its festivals have not remained removed from the tensions of these polarized and antagonistic prospects.[16]

The ensuing theatrical movements move back and forth on this continuum between following the cultural trends of Europe and attempting to establish a purely Latin American form.

Carlos Solórzano divides the early-twentieth-century Latin American drama into four periods, in *Teatro latinoamericano en el siglo XX* (*Latin American Theatre in the Twentieth Century*): *costumbre* (a form of bourgeois domestic comedy), universalist, nationalist, and postwar drama. Solórzano stresses that he covers the *costumbre* form in his book, not because it has any great dramatic value, but because it is the first dramatic form that is uniquely Latin American.[17] The *costumbre*, which encompasses much of the dramatic literature written in the first three decades of the twentieth century, developed out of the tastes of an emerging middle class. The form heralds the first representation of the mestizo characters on stage.

Initially, the *costumbre* took the form of farce, or comedy of manners, in which the stupid or greedy characters in the daily lives of common people were mocked. However, the form soon became an epic of the common man struggling against the ills of society. Solórzano notes that this form marked a shift in national sensibility as the culture of immigrants and indigenous alike blended to form a mestizo culture:

> In each of the countries the mestizaje, the absorption of the indigenous population or the influence of the European immigrants, motivates in the beginning of this century the formation of a particular sensibility and of different forms of expression.... The popular forms, local color, verbal expressions of each country, were captured in comedias and farces, in which the author was given license to make sport of the defects of the society in which he lived.[18]

Although the *costumbre* form seemed to offer meaningless entertainment, it fulfilled a needed function of the new nation. Solórzano felt that while the farcical nature of the *costumbre* originally presented the negative aspects of the middle class, ultimately the *costumbre* gave the growing middle class audience characters with whom they could identify. Most important, the practice of portraying the local language and the customs of the common people carries over into much of the later nationalist drama.

Solórzano defines the next period of Latin American theatre as universalist. Coinciding with the decades following the First World War and the Spanish Civil War, the movement was led by artists who were inspired by the themes and forms used by Europeans. Many Latin American dramatists visited Europe and witnessed the productions of the European avant-garde. Several of the plays of this period contain elements of naturalism and expressionism. The use of unconventional writing and staging also influenced the nationalist drama to come.

Solórzano's third classification of twentieth-century drama is nationalist. The nationalist dramas of the twentieth century have formed in part as a response to foreign imperialism. The United States and other countries of the economic center have a long and complicated history of intervention, both economic and military, in Latin America. The struggles against foreign imperialism have taken many shapes; the drive for national culture has a history just as varied. Nonetheless, because national culture supports the basic formation of a national identity, the works that emerge have some basic themes and ideas in common. The drama of a nation forms and reflects the ideas of the citizens/audience members and helps them identify their fellow citizens and their enemies, know their history, and understand what they believe as a people.

At the beginning of the century, U.S. companies saw economic opportunity in the yet-to-be-developed countries of Latin America. The executives of fruit, cotton, and sugar companies knew that there was money to be made by investing in trade with Latin America. United States–run railroads, telegraph companies, and banks soon followed, along with a sizable debt for Latin America. The United States profited even more from tax-free operation and employment of local workers at substandard wages, much like the free trade zones of today. The United States' prerogative was to invade the Central American countries whenever U.S. companies' economic interests were threatened.

After the cold war, the other great concern of U.S. foreign policy makers was the fear of the spread of communism. Imperialist desires for economic stability combined with anti-Communist fervor to create a U.S. foreign policy in Latin America that tended to favor political stability at all costs. This has led the United States to support some of the bloodiest dictators in history, including Chile's Pinochet, Cuba's Bautista, Nicaragua's Somoza, and Guatemala's Ríos Montt.

Because of the U.S. role in Latin American history, Yankee characters continually appear in Latin American nationalist drama. In dramas that do not include Yankee characters, the United States often hangs as a presence threatening the very essence of the nation. In any case, the drive for the definition of the nation takes on all the more urgency under the threat of foreign domination. From "Abdala" (1869), the short dramatic poem that the Cuban José Martí penned in the mid-nineteenth century, to the most recent works of the Sandinista Revolution, some similar themes emerge about the character of each Latin American nation as people struggle to define themselves against that threat.

Solórzano's fourth and final classification of Latin American drama coincides with the decades following the Second World War. For Solórzano, this postwar drama signals a return to universal ideas instead of local, national ones in an attempt to find, after the horrors of the war, a new moral order and to regenerate humankind.[19]

Dramatists of both Guatemala and Nicaragua have had to struggle to establish and retain any sense of a national culture. Although the Catholic church impeded the development of theatre, Guatemalan and Nicaraguan indigenous performance survived both in the ritual dance drama and in the hybrid, mestizo forms. Both countries have suffered long periods of partisan warfare between urban liberal and agrarian conservative factions. When Guatemala and Nicaragua did gain independence, they found U.S. imperialism to be a far more insidious impediment to nation building. Nicaragua and Guatemala have had varying degrees of success in making national drama part of the national program.

Dramatists in Guatemala and Nicaragua have used diverse methods to develop and disperse the national theatre. However, the themes that the nationalist plays express are similar, as I outline in the following chapters. Also, nationalist performances deploy signs to perform the collective nation in comparable ways. The audience of the national drama comes together, if only in the mind of the playwright, to agree upon the configuration of the nation and to attest to its history. To understand the ways in which the nation is performed, it is necessary to understand the ways in which the nation is constructed.

2 NATIONALISM AND THE PERFORMANCE OF THE NATION

Ay Nicaragua, Nicaragüita
la flor más linda de mi querer
abonada con la bendita,
Nicaragüita,
sangre de Diriangén.[1]
Ay Nicaragua sos[2] *más dulcita*
que la mielita de Tamagás,
pero ahora que ya sos libre, Nicaragüita,
yo te quiero mucho más.
(Nicaragua, Little Nicaragua,
The brightest flower of my love.
Fed with the blessed blood, Little Nicaragua,
of Diriangén.
Oh, Little Nicaragua, you are much sweeter
than the honey of Tamagás.
But now that you are free, Little Nicaragua,
I love you even more.)
   —Carlos Mejía Godoy, *Anthem of the Sandinista Revolution*

The rise in theatrical activity at the outset of any nationalist movement supports the idea that a nation is the performance of nationness. For to revise any notion of what the nation is or should be requires an intense amount of rehearsal, performance, and, ultimately, public agreement. What revolution has there been in which anthems, flags, customs, and other symbols have not been changed, replaced, or redefined?

The national theatre plays a large role in this refiguring for several reasons. National theatre presents an image of the nation to its citizens.

National theatre can effectively re-create the national history. It creates a public forum that both fixes the audience's gaze at the action while calling attention to its public nature. It forms an institution that makes up one of the cultural pillars of the nation; however, the theatre also calls citizens together to agree upon the re-creation of the nation's culture and history.

The Rise of Nationalism

The cycle in Latin American drama, which Solórzano identifies as a cycle from local to universal to local, perhaps indicates the tension between national and regional movements. The body of intellectual writing in Latin America belies a strong regionalist tendency, yet none of the most famous regionalist writers can ever completely turn away from the nationalist cause. In *Imagined Communities,* Benedict Anderson highlights the persistence of nationalism for Marx when he penned in the *Communist Manifesto:* "Though not in substance, yet in form, the struggle of the proletariat with the bourgeoisie is at first a national struggle. The proletariat of each country must, of course, first of all settle matters with its own bourgeoisie."[3] Anderson's point is that Marx never explains why he speaks of a national bourgeoisie. The "of course" makes natural that a world class would be divided by national borders. I suggest the fact that this quote interrupts the continuity of Marx's discussion of a class war and further indicates that Marx takes this point for granted.

Regionalism developed naturally out of Latin America's history, particularly in Central America, where five countries (Guatemala, Honduras, El Salvador, Nicaragua, and Costa Rica) were once part of a larger federation. As Timothy Brennen points out, certain factors, such as "unities of language, common enemies, and . . . contiguous terrain," bolster the regionalist intellectualism of writers such as Cuba's José Martí.[4] But even as Martí writes about America, he also paints a vivid and passionate picture of what it means to be a Cuban. Martí sets Cuba apart from other Latin American nations. He can clearly name characteristics of the Cuban citizen in opposition to those who are not Cuban. Eduardo Galeano felt the same tension. An Uruguayan who fought for Guatemalan rebel forces, Galeano often wrote that the fight against imperialism had to be fought on a continental scale against an enemy, the United States, who dominated an entire region. But he carefully cautions his reader:

> Yet there are important differences between some Latin American countries and others, and thoughts and actions must be based on the realization that a

single formula cannot apply to different situations. It would be a serious mistake to confuse Guatemala's largely Indian, peasant, and illiterate society with the cosmopolitan and predominantly middle-class society of Uruguay.[5]

How then does the nation persist, when regionalism continually tempers the nationalist ideas of Latin America?

The nation is not real, nor is it imaginary. The nation resides somewhere between fact and construct, somewhere between the physical geography and the concept agreed upon by the people who count themselves as citizens. The crises caused by the lack of legitimacy, as in the cases of Kuwait or Yugoslavia, attest to the nation's constructedness. The insistence on its legitimacy, as in the case of Poland time and again, attests to its realness. The nation is more than land, but it is much more than mere metaphor.

Anderson and Bhabha have both pointed out that the concept of the nation developed relatively recently. In order for us to visualize ourselves as part of a group beyond what we can physically see in this field or in that village, certain criteria must be met. In *Nations and Nationalism*, Ernest Gellner suggests that those criteria lie within the transition of society from agrarian to industrial. The same social forces that allow for the restructuring of society for industry create the grounds for the idea of a unit based on shared culture. Gellner states that people make up a nation who "share the same culture" and who "recognize each other as belonging to the same nation."[6] Shared culture alone does not meet the criteria to create the sense of nationhood. For Gellner, that culture must be transmitted through a series of institutions: specifically, a large, centralized education system. Such a series of institutions are too large to be maintained by very small groups, which creates the need for smaller cultures to be absorbed, through force or by choice, into larger, high cultures.

In *Imagined Communities*, Anderson focuses on the phenomenon of print media with respect to the rise of the idea of nation. Because many nations contain vastly diverse cultures, shared culture is more imagined than actually transmitted. Anderson uses the newspaper to illustrate this imagined community moving through "homogenous, empty time:"[7] A citizen of a nation reads a newspaper that contains information about what fellow citizens are doing. At the same time, the citizen imagines that others of the same nation are engaged in the same ritual of reading the same news. The wide dissemination of printed material does more than define the shared culture or the shared language. It actually creates the sense of nation within the imagination of the citizen. A nation becomes a "solid community moving steadily down (or up) history."[8]

In the Latin American colonies, criollos felt a sense of separateness from the Iberian Peninsula because they were excluded from the privileges granted to the European-born. Anderson explains that political careers of criollos involved movement within the defined boundaries of their territory to the economic center of a particular colony. But criollos were still barred from holding the highest posts, which were reserved for European-born Spaniards. This exclusion, combined with the predetermined geographical limit to their appointments, created a sense of the colony as a bounded country separated from Spain. According to Anderson, the nation was not fully realized until local newspapers created a sense of coherent reality among the literate criollo class.[9] By the time the criollo nationalists felt compelled to break away from the world from which they were excluded, there was a sense of regional solidarity in Latin America that existed nowhere else. However, the rise of print-capitalism defined more clearly the boundaries that were already created by colonial precedent.

The dual phenomena of exclusion from Spanish citizenship and visualization of a community worked together to form an idea of the Latin American nation. Citizens view the nation in terms of what or who lies within the nation, as well as what or who lies without. The colonial criollos were excluded from citizenship of the Iberian Peninsula and were acutely aware of what was *"nuestra"* America and what was not. In a similar manner, nationalists of countries plagued with excessive foreign influence have a keen sense of where the boundary of citizenship lies. When Gellner talks about the relationship of industrialization to nationalism he suggests:

> As the tidal wave of modernization sweeps the world, it makes sure that almost everyone, at some time or other, has cause to feel unjustly treated, and that he can identify the culprits as being of another "nation." If he can also identify enough of the victims as being of the same "nation" as himself, a nationalism is born. If it succeeds, and not all of them can, a nation is born.[10]

As the colonies industrialized, the "culprits" in the case of Central America generally came from the United States, and nationalist sentiment grew out of the desire to expel the foreign capitalists.

The U.S. capitalists and the Marines who usually accompanied them appear in several of the nationalist dramas, and the plots often involve the uniting of the people of the nation against them. *El tren amarillo* features A. Tom Bomb and his agent Mr. Whip. *Por los caminos van los campesinos* involves a U.S. Marine who rapes the *campesino*'s daughter; and Rolando Steiner's *Pájaros del norte* involves a U.S. Marine who marries and then abandons the daughter of that family. The United States appears in *Banana Republic* as simply the character Imperialismo. These characters create a needed unifying factor in light of the diversity within the community being created.

The National Race

In the creation of the boundaries of the nation, which mark who belongs within the nation and who belongs without, race provides nationalists with a challenge. Although Anderson only glosses race, writers of colonized nations write at length on race and nation. The Algerian nationalist Frantz Fanon equates race and nation when he writes about Algeria in *The Wretched of the Earth*. For Fanon, there was an essential distinction between those who were Algerian and those who did not belong: "decolonization is quite simply the replacing of a certain 'species' of men by another 'species' of men."[11] The invasion of the colonizing Other carried severe emotional as well as political consequences. But in Algeria, the division between colonizer and colonized was a clear racial boundary. Latin American writers who take their cue from Fanon wrestle with race, an issue that is not as clear-cut in nations with racially diverse populations.

In her book on the romance novels of Latin America, Doris Sommer observes how the complex ideas of race and nation weave together:

> Miscegenation was the road to racial perdition in Europe, but it was the way of redemption in Latin America, a way of annihilating difference and constructing a deeply horizontal, fraternal dream of national identity. It was a way of imagining the nation through a future history, like a desire that works through time and yet derives its irresistible power from *feeling* natural and ahistorical.[12]

Often the writers of the national drama use the figures of mixed-race people as symbols of the emerging nation.

The Cuban writer Roberto Fernández Retamar refers to *mestizaje*—the blending of the three principal races of black, white, and indigenous—as essentially American.[13] But, Central American dramatists often struggle to create a view of the diverse nation and of the Central Americans as a "race." Often nationalist writers appropriate the figure of the mestizo. The drama and literature of the twentieth century began to reflect mestizos as mestizo people began to constitute part of the rising middle class.

Use of the national drama to create the insider/outsider boundary, with the construction of a national race and the expulsion of the imperialist Other, helps solidify the national identity. For instance, the Guatemalan playwright Manuel Galich writes about the multiracial poor of the Caribbean coast in the 1957 drama *El tren amarillo*. They are marked as the "true" Guatemalans in a struggle against the Yankee banker, A. Tom Bomb. Racism is discussed by the planters, who view racism as an imported evil from the United States. However, the Chinese character Mariano, a Guatemalan-born merchant, also finds himself on the list of outsiders. Galich betrays the Guatemalan sentiment that the Chinese are a symptom of U.S. imperialism because the United Fruit Company brought many Chinese laborers to build the railroads. Mariano's presence draws a clear line between those who are Guatemalan and those who are not.

In a similar vein, the indigenous people of Latin America appear in nationalist drama as a symbol of what is naturally Latin American. That is, dramatists invoke the concept of *mestizaje* to create the sense that all people of a Latin American nation belong to the nation by natural inheritance. The line where Nicaragua is fed by the "sangre de Diriangén" in the Sandinista national anthem points to the Nicaraguans' natural descent from the indigenous people of the region. The resurgence of interest in the culture of the Guatemalan Mayas in the middle of the twentieth century in the plays of Asturias attests to an identification with the original people of Guatemala.

National History

Creating a shared sense of culture also entails creating a shared sense of history. The citizen views the community as "moving steadily down history." The community's history, therefore, forms one of the significant boundaries of that community. National drama retells the history of the nation for the audience and creates a sense of a people having shared the trial of attaining independence together. However, in the same way that the nation resides between construct and fact, so, too, does history.

Scholarship on nationalism suggests that nationalist movements continually engage in refiguring a nation's past. Anderson suggests that one of the paradoxes of nationalist thought is the "objective modernity of nations to the historian's eye [versus] their subjective antiquity in the eyes of nationalists."[14] In *The Invention of Tradition,* Hobsbawm follows a similar line of thought: "It is clear that plenty of political institutions, ideological movements and groups—not least in nationalism—were so unprecedented that even historical continuity had to be invented."[15] As nationalists reconfigure the nation, they must reconfigure the national history.

Part of the project of the nationalist dramatist is to construct a shared national history to be performed and recognized by the theatre audience. Play texts, then, refigure past events as recognizable and logical precursors to the present. The national history reflects the present configuration of the country. Group recognition of the shared past creates the sense of the "real" nation as having come forward into the present from the past and the sense that the nation, and its history, is eternal.

Nationalist Culture

The theatre provides an excellent vehicle for the performance of the nation. In her examination of British, French, and U.S. nationalist theatre in *The National Stage*, Loren Kruger asserts that "the idea of representing the nation in the theatre, of summoning a representative audience that will in turn recognize itself," is a compelling and problematic phenomenon.[16] The public nature of theatre creates a forum in which an audience may visibly and publicly recognize or contest the image of the nation on stage and can thereby legitimate the notion of the nation in a way that individual readers of a novel or a newspaper cannot. Diana Taylor asserts that the public spectacle is an ideal forum for the imagining of communities.[17] For postcolonial nations, the historical nature of a nationalist play provides for the audience a reenactment of the story of how the nation emerged from colonialism and survived the abuse of foreign imperialists: a testimony of the trials to which the people were subjected. The writing of the play memorializes the events as they may be agreed upon by the audience and preserves them in drama for later generations.

However, while first-world nations have histories of ambiguity and contestations of national identity, their identities have not recently been challenged as much as, or in the same way as, those of third-world nations. The identities of Guatemala and Nicaragua in the twentieth century were formed in spite of (by resisting the destructive force of foreign domination) and because of (as the external force makes the citizens of the nation pull more tightly together) the imperialist desires of foreign capitalists, most notably from the United States, which sought to exploit or absorb them.

Also, it is important to note that this performance of the national identity does not occur in isolation. It continues a dialogue of ideas about the character of the nation, as the nation itself is too unstable of a construct to exist outside of this continuous string of repeat performances. Judith Butler writes about the way performance constitutes identity:

> What "performs" does not exhaust the "I"; it does not lay out in visible terms the comprehensive content of that "I," for if the performance is "repeated," there is always the question of what differentiates from each other the moments of identity that are repeated. And if the "I" is the effect of a certain repetition, one which produces the semblance of a continuity or coherence, then there is no "I" that preceded the gender that it is said to perform; the repetition, and the failure to repeat, produce a string of performances that constitute and contest the coherence of that "I."[18]

Although Butler reiterates the way in which feminist and queer theorists use this concept to theorize gender and sexuality, her ideas are also applicable to the concept of national identity.

From the signs that are deployed on a daily basis, such as flags or anthems; to monuments of national history; to onetime events, such as protests or the staging of plays; each works in concert to create a sense of the nation as natural or essential in some way. However, as Butler argues, it is the repetitive and obligatory nature of the performance that gives away its tenuousness. If the performance were natural, it would not need to be continually reaffirmed.

The repetition adds gravity to a cultural practice. In Richard Terdiman's examination of cultural theory, he says of the cultural system:

> Like the economic infrastructure sustaining any social formation, culture is an accumulation. And it achieves its relative stability, its practical weight, its seeming coherence, through its constant rehearsal and reproduction in individual and social memory. The practices of a cultural system ... both function as a memory, and function to ensure its stabilization and transmission.[19]

However, repetition does not guarantee the permanence of the nation. This is why manifestos calling for a national theatre are so impassioned. Pablo Antonio Cuadra called for a theatrical tradition that was uniquely Nicaraguan and argued that a theatre company should be established in every province. Cuadra was responding to what he felt were Yankee influences and the degradation of what was Nicaraguan. The paradox of a theatre based in unique Nicaraguan tradition, in which there had been no formal theatrical tradition, made the desperation to perform that much greater.

In the public venue of the theatre, Anderson's concept of homogenous, empty time is played out in a repeated public ritual, by which the citizen can physically see fellow citizens engaged in the same action of legitimation. Of this audience dynamic Taylor says:

> Individual and state formation take place, in part, in the visual sphere through a complicated play of looks: looking, being looked at, identification, recognition, mimicry. This internal network of looks takes place within the overarching structure of the Lacanian gaze. . . in which we are all objects, all part of the spectacle.[20]

The citizen recognizes other citizens within the audience and recognizes their acts of validation. The citizen can go on from there and imagine the community of the nation following this practice as long as the drama runs and as long as there is a national theatre. These performances, scattered over many spatial and temporal locations, reveal what Homi Bhabha believes is the "image of cultural authority[,] . . . ambivalent because it is caught, uncertainly, in the act of 'composing' its powerful image."[21] The identity of the nation shifts and changes, and the representation of the commonly held images follows changing practices. But the moment of performance projects the image of the unchanging and the eternal. The performances are inconsistent and fragmentary, yet continuous in the drive to create the seamless sense of nation.

The following analysis explores the ways that the nation is defined and performed through nationalist drama. The following chapters examine how the nationalist plays of Guatemala and Nicaragua distinguish the national borders through the establishment of a national race and language, the creation of a national character, and the reconfiguration of the national history. The following playwrights and their plays have been instrumental in helping define and redefine the national culture at critical junctures in those nations' histories.

PART TWO
GUATEMALA: NATIONAL METAPHORS

3   GUATEMALAN NATIONAL THEATRE

Early Guatemalan national history is marred by partisan warfare. The Guatemalan government and the government of the Central American federation tried to maintain a Liberal political program of developing infrastructure and limiting the power of the church. However, in 1838, an illiterate mestizo pig farmer named José Rafael Carrera succeeded in taking back the government for the Conservative interests. He managed to hold power for the Conservative Party until 1871, when the Liberals staged a coup.

The following Liberal regime of Justo Rufino Barrios was just as authoritarian as the Conservative regime, but Barrios focused on building infrastructure. He developed a system of forced labor and began compulsory education, which served to assimilate the indigenous people. The Barrios government focused mainly on developing an economy that could participate more actively in international trade. The Barrios government not only developed the telegraph and postal services in Guatemala but new export crops, such as coffee and cotton, as well. The balance of power between Liberals and Conservatives remained tenuous, and any attempt to tip that balance resulted in more partisan warfare.

Very little national theatre flourished in Guatemala during the time between the Spanish Conquest and the 1944 Revolution. The "mestizo" theatre, what Hugo Carrillo calls a true Guatemalan theatre, did not develop until the twentieth century. Carrillo does say that Spanish theatre companies toured the region after Guatemala's independence from Spain. A theatre was built during Carreras's presidency, and a few playwrights saw their works staged; however, these, Carrillo says, were imitative of Peninsular dramas.

Ismael Cerna wrote the first nationalist drama in Guatemala in 1891.[1] *La penitenciaría* (*The Penitentiary*), a three-act drama in verse, tells the story of a father who asks his son to "give his talents to the enslaved who struggle to break the chains in order to know their rights, and their country, and they will know that 'the God of the Andes protects their liberty.'"[2] The play "contains the exaltations of liberty characteristic of romanticism, honorable liberty in the face of humiliating subjection."[3] Although Carrillo feels that this play has little dramatic value, he does say that the play reflects a "national reality," that it speaks out against the tyranny of Barrios and his successor, and that its political current makes it part of what he calls mestizo theatre.[4]

When one of Barrios's successors attempted to stay in power by force, Conservative conspirators assassinated him, and Manuel Estrada Cabrera took over the government in 1898. In the early years of Cabrera's regime, the *costumbre* genre flourished.

Some of the early works of Manuel Galich fall under the *costumbre* category. Galich wrote a satire, *M'hijo el bachiller* (*My Son the Bachelor*) (1938), a Guatemalan version of Florencio Sánchez's *M'hijo el dotor* (*My Son the Doctor*) (1903), which deals specifically with problems faced by ambitious middle-class parents who attempt to make their children pursue professions for which they are not capable.[5] This work is also Galich's commentary on the education system of Guatemala. A shoemaker, Don Pedro Zapata, takes pride in his son's graduation from college. Mario's professor, Don Chepe, calls Mario an ignoramus and explains to Don Pedro that he was only allowed to graduate because Zapata was well liked and because people really appreciated the fine and inexpensive job he does on their shoes. Galich also employed local idioms in his dramatic writing and often included footnotes and glossaries to explain the common expressions used in the text. In his early work are the seeds of Galich's later nationalist drama, which grew up during the era of increasing economic domination by the United States.

The Conservatives of the early twentieth century developed a program of close association with the United States. The United States backed Cabrera in 1898 when he defaulted on debt owed to Great Britain and aided him against the Mexicans when they invaded in 1907. The economy declined considerably during his regime, as Conservatives paid little attention to the national economy. Massive investments from foreign companies in 1906, specifically from the Boston-based United Fruit Company and its associated railway, kept the Guatemalan economy afloat. It also created a situation in which the better part of the country's resources, both the raw materials and all the shipping, were in the hands of foreign capitalists.

Cabrera viciously repressed any opposition by having his opponents assassinated or imprisoned. Cabrera's regime deteriorated gradually as his paranoia worsened. He eventually shut himself off from contact with others and would only eat food prepared by his mother. The U.S. Congress intervened in 1920, declaring Cabrera mentally unfit to run the government, and appointed his successor. Although the United States effectively deposed him, Cabrera had a significant impact on the formation of cultural identity. Miguel Ángel Asturias modeled the title character in his Nobel Prize–winning novel *El señor presidente* (*Mr. President*) (1946) after the dictator.

Although no writer dared to stage anything critical of Cabrera, several Guatemalan playwrights began to experiment with language, writing plays that were more poetic than narrative. One of Guatemala's most popular playwrights, Adolfo Drago Bracco, continued to write entertaining comedies and plays that dealt with issues pressing to the mestizo bourgeoisie, and he perfected Guatemalan dramatic writing and gave depth and range to dramatic characters.[6]

The work of Miguel Masicovetere y Durán (1912–) shows a strong Italian influence and is indicative of the influence of theatre of the grotesque in Guatemalan writing. His play *La mujer y el robot* (*The Woman and the Robot*) (1930) depicts the destruction of the world by machines. Although Masicovetere founded the Grupo Tepeus in 1930, his work was not often staged because there was so little theatrical activity in Guatemala. Solórzano feels that his work

> signifies, in this moment, the intersection [of Latin American drama] with good Western theatre after the Second World War. And this was achieved by its character of science fiction and its biological explanation of the most complex psychological dimensions, resembling in its execution plays of O'Neil [*sic*] such as *Dynamo* and *The Hairy Ape*.[7]

Where the writers of the *costumbre* brought to the stage local themes important to the national bourgeoisie, later dramatists attempted to perfect the craft of playwrighting and to explore new forms. The *costumbres* had addressed domestic issues and had portrayed the successes and failures of a class. Now the universalist drama was influenced by expressionism and surrealism and tended to deal with either the struggle of humans against an increasingly technological world or the nature of human consciousness. Both of these forms influenced the nationalist drama that was to come.

The Revolutionary Culture

After a series of Conservative presidents, Jorge Ubico was elected in 1930. Ubico had very close ties to the United States, and hoped the United States would back him if he tried to forcefully reunify Central America. He attempted to claim British Honduras (now Belize) and launched covert operations against the leaders of El Salvador and Honduras. Ubico was reluctant to take action against Germans, who held land during the Second World War, because Guatemala was actually doing good business with Germany in the coffee trade. However, Ubico seized German plantations in 1944. By this time, there was a growing nationalist sentiment to seize all foreign-held land, and a general strike in 1944 forced Ubico to resign. Because Ubico's actions alienated the usually supportive United States, the U.S. government did nothing to intervene.

During this time, Manuel Galich made a transition from writing *costumbres* to writing nationalist drama. Although Galich's *costumbres* were critical of the middle class, his nationalist dramas take aim at foreign corporations. He also criticizes the opportunistic Guatemalans who do business with them. Galich's *costumbres* focused on middle-class mestizos and their families, but the nationalist dramas forge a horizontal fellowship with people from various classes and of various ethnic backgrounds.

During the democratic regimes between Guatemala's 1944 revolution and the 1954 U.S. invasion, the revolutionary government founded several new cultural institutions. According to Carrillo, the General Office of Fine Arts, the Popular University, the Faculty of Humanities, and the Indigenous Institute were all founded after 1944. The state also aided in the founding of schools of dramatic art, the establishment of art and cultural festivals, the organization of competitions, and the construction of a national theatre on the outskirts of Guatemala City.[8]

After Guatemalan students' successful strike and revolt in 1944, the democratically elected administrations of Juan José Arévalo and Jacobo Arbenz made the mistake of embarking on a policy of agricultural reform. This pitted the Guatemalan government against the United Fruit Company, which had a rather impressive monopoly on banana cultivation and export.

Although Guatemala had been relatively free of direct military intervention by the United States, United Fruit aggressively moved into the Caribbean banana market and pushed out many small planters in the process. By the 1930s, United Fruit controlled the International Railways of Central America (IRCA, which was a subsidiary) and owned Guatemala's only Caribbean port, Puerto Barrios. It was impossible to export bananas without dealing with United Fruit. By controlling trade, United Fruit was able to obtain some of the best land and to become the largest grower in Guatemala.

Both Cabrera and Ubico had showed United Fruit tremendous favor. They allowed United Fruit to declare a depreciated value on its agricultural holdings in order to pay exceedingly low taxes. Ubico had enacted measures to keep wages of workers low across the country in order to prevent United Fruit's workers from striking.

The Arévalo and Arbenz governments (especially the Arbenz administration) attempted to collect property taxes owed by the company. Arbenz was interested primarily in agricultural reform, which would make Guatemala more economically stable. Some large land holdings were redistributed to landless peasants to form cooperatives. The land was paid for with government bonds. In a radical move, Arbenz offered to pay United Fruit the value it declared on the land, a value significantly less than its real value. United Fruit executives could either pay the taxes the company owed or give up some of its holdings for a radically depreciated value.

The United States, in particular Central Intelligence Agency (CIA) Director Allan Dulles, viewed the democratic regime as hostile to U.S. interests. By 1954, the CIA had mobilized disaffected Guatemalans and had organized a United States–supported military coup. The CIA generated popular support in the United States for the coup by painting the Arbenz administration as Communist. Daniel James mused, in 1954, in *Red Design for the Americas:*

> While president, Arbenz vehemently insisted that he was no Communist. But very few literate Guatemalans doubted exactly where he stood. It may be said of him, in fact, that during his Presidency he did more than any other man to further the Soviet conspiracy.[9] . . . Long before Arbenz became a candidate for President, his home had been converted by María (Arbenz' wife) into a Marxist salon. It was peopled by Red intellectuals from all over.[10]

The CIA used the fear of communism to launch a coup that would return control of the country to regimes friendlier to the likes of United Fruit.

After the United States–backed 1954 coup, dramatists continued to pursue national and regional themes, but they avoided any direct political criticism of the regime. Often, their dramas showed the effects of tyranny on the souls of its protagonists without directly criticizing the dictatorship itself.

Hugo Carrillo's (1928–1994) first play, *La calle del sexo verde* (*The Street of Smut*[11]) (1959) falls into this category. The play caused a stir when it premiered at the first Guatemalan theatre festival at the Universidad Popular in Guatemala City. The play was controversial because it presented a homosexual character, and it raised the issue of abortion. Although this was probably the first Guatemalan play to feature a homosexual character, the play presents homosexuality as a perversion that results from the young man's abuse and the corruption of society in general. In Carrillo's play, homosexuality is viewed as more of a social problem than a legitimate sexual identity.

Carrillo's next play, *El corazón del espantapájaros* (*The Heart of the Scarecrow*) (1961), derives from Shakespeare's *Hamlet*. As a political statement, the players of *Hamlet* act out the play-within-a-play to reveal the "conscience of the king." Carrillo gave the play a Brechtian staging using songs and masks. He was also known for his adaptation of Asturias's Nobel Prize–winning novel *El Señor Presidente* (*Mr. President*) for the stage in 1974.

Manuel José Arce utilized the history of Nicaragua to raise Guatemalan national issues in his drama ¡*Viva Sandino!* (*Sandino Lives!*). The first part of the drama, *Sandino debe nacer* (*Sandino Must Be Born*) (1975), has an ensemble cast covering the entire history of Nicaragua to the birth of Sandino. The play presents the history rhetorically, bringing the audience to the conclusion that Nicaragua, and by extension Guatemala, needs a liberator such as Augusto Sandino. The other two plays of the trilogy, *Sandino debe morir* (*Sandino Must Die*) and *Sandino debe vivir* (*Sandino Must Live*), mentioned in ¡*Viva Sandino!*, were either written and not published, or have not been written at all.

The writers of Guatemalan drama offer a series of metaphors that attempt to define the borders of the nation. The metaphors provide a glimpse into who these writers see as the ideal Guatemalan, how they visualize the national race, and who belongs within or outside the nation.

National Metaphors

The citizens/audience members hold within their minds specific borders that map out the nation and define not only the nature of the nation but also who shares the culture and who does not. These borders fluctuate. In *Theatre Audiences,* Susan Bennett discusses how culture frames an audience member's reaction to a text. She suggests:

Both an audience's reaction to a text (or performance) and the text (performance) itself are bound within cultural limits. Yet, as diachronic analysis makes apparent, those limits are continually tested and invariably broken. Culture cannot be held as a fixed entity, a set of constant rules, but instead it must be seen as in a position of inevitable flux.[12]

As the feeling of nationhood is built upon the idea of a supposed shared culture, the same applies to the current configuration of the nation, the limits of which change continually. At the same time, however, a culture or a nation must appear stable.

Because of the instability of these imaginings, we cannot define what the nation is in the imaginations of all the citizens all of the time. However, by examining the kinds of metaphors that occur in drama written as part of a nationalist project, we can understand where some of the boundaries lie at least at that moment the play is written and/or performed.

A dramatic metaphor for the nation may involve several elements, such as the specific map of the nation. Spatial metaphors on stage help to structure the audience's identification of the boundaries, real or imagined, of the nation. For example, the setting for the play, or a place that has a specific cultural significance, may represent the location of the nation. Within a setting such as a house or a family, the audience can physically see those contained within the nation and those outside of it. Also, a playwright may personify the nation through a specific character: either the protagonist or a character through which the protagonist/citizen encounters the moral dilemma that defines his or her citizenship.

For example, in Nicaragua the Sandinista national anthem refers to Nicaragua as "Nicaragüita," a term that signifies that something is little or dear. The song recognizes Nicaragua as "the brightest flower of my love" and tells the nation "but now that you are free, I love you even more." The Sandinistas wrote a love song to their nation to be sung at every significant event. The Sandinistas drew fire for their close associations of romantic love with the nation when they ran advertisements picturing two youths in love that referred to how special a first love is as a way to ensure that young people exercised their first vote in 1990. The act of participating in the governing of the nation was equated with the consummation of that romantic love.

The metaphor of the family as the nation works in two ways. On the one hand, the family on stage serves as a microcosm of all the families of the nation. It stands in for every family, and therefore every citizen, and reflects the thoughts, feelings, and values that the audience considers representative of the thoughts, feelings, and values of every family in the nation.

On the other hand, the stage family serves as a laboratory to observe the effects of society on the individual. The political developments of the nation are reflected in the generational conflicts of the family. The family plays out on stage any tension or struggle over the national identity. Several of the writers discussed here provide the audience with what is to serve as the "typical" Nicaraguan or Guatemalan family. Pablo Antonio Cuadra paints a vivid picture of the Nicaraguan peasant family in *Por los caminos van los campesinos*. Miguel Ángel Asturias captures the household of Guatemalan newlyweds in *Soluna*. Manuel Galich follows a single mother and her son through the history of the economic domination by United Fruit in *El tren amarillo*. In all of these plays, members of each family demonstrate ideas of national race, language, and culture.

Actor Marta Meneses-Mendoza dances with a red scarf in a scene about the reality that women face in making decisions about sexual and reproductive health. Each of the three women in the play *Al ritmo del tambor de la vida* (To the Beat of the Drum of Life) is faced with the prospect of an abortion. Wisconsin Coordinating Council on Nicaragua.

Three women talk while doing their washing in a scene about women and their relationships with their daughters. *El espejo* (The Mirror). Wisconsin Coordinating Council on Nicaragua.

The silhouette of Sandino on "La Loma."

Courtesy of Eduardo Manfut Provedor. http://www.manfut.org.

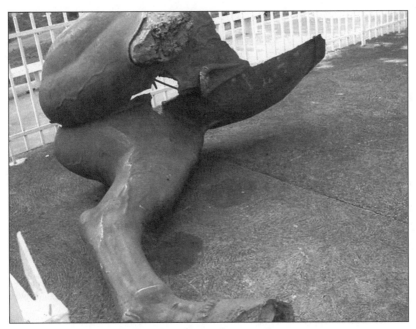

The statue fragment at the feet of Sandino on "La Loma."
Courtesy of Eduardo Manfut Provedor. http://www.manfut.org.

Our Land Is Made of Courage and Glory mural, a full view of the plaza. Author's collection.

Our Land Is Made of Courage and Glory mural, Sandino's silhouette and the last letter of Rigoberto López Pérez. Author's collection.

Our Land Is Made of Courage and Glory mural, Fonseca's glasses. Author's collection.

Our Land Is Made of Courage and Glory mural, Somoza bricks. Author's collection.

Our Land Is Made of Courage and Glory mural, horse's rear. Author's collection.

4 MANUEL GALICH AND *MESTIZAJE*

In a few of the plays, the variable of race strengthens the insider/outsider boundary drawn by the contrast between essentially native characters and brutal foreigners. As the Latin American states began to develop a sense of national identity, the conceptualization of the ethnic basis for each nation and for the region began to shift. The colonial government had created an elaborate racial hierarchy based on the percentage of a race that constituted a person's ethnic background. The Europeans, who occupied the top of this racial pyramid, and the criollos, who occupied the small space below the top, testified to the racism of colonial Spain to the point that white men born in the Americas were somehow tainted by association. Eventually, as the Latin American nations matured, the United States began to play a major role in the formation of a national and regional ethnic identity. The concept shifted from one of a superior race governing savages toward the more progressive notion of a Latin American "race" protecting itself from Yankee imperialists.

According to Etienne Balibar, racism spins off from nationalism and also constitutes it in some ways. In fact, Balibar believes, racism strengthens nationalism against some of the inherent contradictions that exist between it and universality, which may provide some insight into how Latin American regionalism and nationalism exist despite the tension between them. Balibar asserts of racism:

> The excess it represents in relation to nationalism, and therefore the supplement it brings to it, tends both to universalize it, to correct its lack of universality, and to particularize it, to correct its lack of specificity. In other words, racism actually adds to the ambiguous nature of nationalism, which means that, through racism, nationalism engages in a "headlong fight forward," a metamorphosis of its material conditions into ideal contradictions.[1]

European anti-Semitism operates regionally, as white supremacists react against a perceived outsider, a scapegoat for economic difficulties and political turmoil. In a postcolonial twist of this notion, the anti–United States sentiment in Latin America works to forge Latin American national unity in the unifying moniker "our America." Where Europeans create nationalist sentiments out of constructions of racial purity, Latin Americans unite behind a mythos of racial solidarity.

This does not mean that the previous concept of the racial hierarchy does not exist in Latin America; it does. But it exists in dynamic tension with newer, progressive ideas of a mestizo or multiracial Latin American people fighting to expel blond U.S. Marines from Latin American soil. This tension adds a contentious element to the deployment of the national character in the national drama. For, as Tamara Underiner argues in *Cultures Enacted/Cultures in Action: (Intercultural) Theatre in Mayan Mexico,* the indigenous component of the *mestizaje* equation is almost always appropriated, or even assimilated, by the dominant class, which produces the national high culture, while the political reality remains that the indigenous people occupy the bottom tier of the hierarchy.[2]

Although race figures directly into some of the play texts, race forms the background of others. In western Central America, the *costumbre* genre featured the mestizo family as the mestizos gained some economic power as part of an emerging middle class. Nicaraguan texts such as *Por los caminos van los campesinos* and Hernán Robleto's *Pájaros del norte* (*Birds of the North*) (1936) do not identify the race of all the characters, but rather than leave them unmarked, as they are in nineteenth-century criollo dramas, a few nonwhite characters are represented. In the dialogue of *Pájaros del norte,* the character Enrique mentions that people say he is inferior because of his darker color, and he specifically points out that the character María is criollo when he says "dark woman of the criollo race, little dark woman who doesn't see the danger of the men who come speaking English."[3] When Chon and María do their hair as they prepare to go out, Chon remarks that she has switched hair treatments because one makes her hair dark. As the play is set during the U.S. occupation of Nicaragua, the trend to look fair follows the trend of catching a Yankee husband. Robleto criticizes racism and links it directly to the U.S. presence in Nicaragua.

By the mid-twentieth century, the issue of *mestizaje* became much more complex than dark or light, indigenous or criollo. While immigrants from all over the world moved to Latin America, the racial issues demanded more thoughtful attention from the national dramatist. The most interesting attempt to address this racial complexity appears in

Manuel Galich's *El tren amarillo* (*The Yellow Train*), a play about the oppression of Guatemala by the United Fruit Company.

From *Costumbrismo* to Political Activism

Manuel Galich López showed an interest in the theatre at an early age. He was born in Guatemala City in 1913. His aunt María Magdalena López (on his mother's side) was an actress and ran a children's theatre company in the 1920s and 1930s. Galich and his family attended the theatre frequently, and he began writing plays when he was in college.

Galich seemed destined both to be a teacher and to have a career in politics. Galich's writing reflects his training in both; he wrote plays that reflected the political situation in Guatemala as well as plays for children about Guatemalan culture. Galich went to work at the young age of eleven in the law office of Viteri, Silva, and Falla. He left the job in 1928 when he received a scholarship for the Escuela Normal Central de Varones, a teacher's college. Galich excelled in his studies and showed promise as a scholar and orator: he won a district-wide speech competition in 1930. A general strike by the teachers at the college interrupted his studies in 1931. Galich later transferred to the Instituto Nacional Central de Varones and received his bachelor's degree in primary education. While Galich was working toward his degree, he began to write plays for the stage. Little is known about his first play, written in 1932, *Los conspiradores* (*The Conspirators*), and it seems that it was never staged.

Although Galich received his degree in education, he entered the law school at his alma mater in 1933. Increasing repression by the Guatemalan government and exposure to new ideas in the law school gave Galich the impetus to become involved in the struggle against Ubico. Galich was outspoken and began organizing his classmates and colleagues. The students demanded that the university, which was under government control, be made autonomous. They called for the resignation of several of the university officials tied to the regime. More than once, Galich had to answer questions in the police station, and in 1940 he was suspended from the school for a statement he made against Ubico's reelection.

In spite of the suspension, Galich continued to organize. He became director of the group El Derecho (The Right), and formed the Asociación de Estudiante Universitarios (Association of University Students, or AEU). The AEU played an important role in the Day of the Student, September 15, 1943, a day that marks the beginning of the revolution. In 1944 a general strike started by students and professors forced Ubico, and later his predecessor, Ponce Vaides, from power. Galich's instrumental role in the revolution of 1944 was rewarded by the new president, Arévalo, who appointed Galich Minister of Education.

In his new role, Galich incorporated Guatemalan culture and history into the school curriculum, including Mayan culture and history. His action marked a shift away from a curriculum geared toward Spanish as the privileged culture and toward a nationalist agenda of glorifying Guatemalan culture and its place within Central American culture.

During these early years, Galich wrote the first play of his trilogy on the Natas family. *Papá Natas* (Father Natas, or more accurately, *The Gullible*) (1938), a political satire, criticizes the Ubico regime. The play takes place after the U.S. stock market crash of 1929. Guatemalan families were all feeling the effects of the fallout because of Guatemala's economic relationship with the United States.

Lolo (Papá) Natas finds himself out of work until a corrupt government official, Marcos López, offers him a position as district administrator. Because her father is overjoyed at the news, Eva Natas cannot refuse the advances of López, a man she despises. Eva knows that her compliance is a condition of her father's employment.

Galich sticks to the conventions of realism in his early work. He uses the Guatemalan middle class to reflect the current national issues. But where *M'hijo el bachiller* follows the domestic drama format and remains fairly unified in time, place, and action, *Papá Natas* reveals the beginnings of Galich's later epic style. He abandons the short, more neoclassical timeline for action that spans several years. Galich also uses presentational elements. At the beginning of act 1, scene 3, for instance, sirens are heard over Morse code and teletype machines, and the music of the Charleston. Actors shout out headlines:

> Tuesday, October 29, 1929! Panic spreads in the New York stock market! 10 A.M. At the opening of transactions, the number of sales rises to more than three million. 12 dazzling hours![4]

After describing the crash of the stock market, the background noise stops. The actors pause before taking up headlines about the fallout from the crash in a more monotone style. This sets the stage for the impact of the Depression on the Natas family.

Galich also wrote dramas for children. With his training in primary education, Galich felt that it was a necessity to create dramatic presentations that helped children understand Guatemalan national history and culture, and Mayan culture in particular. One of the first of these plays, *El Señor Gukup Cakix* (*Mr. Gukup Cakix*) (1939) was based on the Mayan Popul Vuh, an ancient collection of the Mayan creation myths.

In the 1940s, Galich wrote several short pedagogical plays based on historical themes. One of the first was *Belem, 1813* (1940), a play about the conspirators of Belem, one of the first fights for Central American independence. The play depicts a meeting of the conspirators to plan a rebellion against the colonial government. In the end, the conspirators are betrayed by one of the group and handed over to colonial soldiers. He also wrote *15 de Septiembre* (*The Fifteenth of September*) about a debate among Guatemala's "founding fathers" before signing the document declaring Guatemalan independence in 1821. These didactic pieces were staged in 1940 as part of Galich's rhetorical struggle against the dictatorship.

Galich returned to the Natas family in 1953 with *La mugre* (*The Filth*). This time Galich used the Natas family to criticize what Galich felt were traitorous elements within the revolutionary government. The corruption within the family mirrors the corruption in the Guatemalan government. The play follows Arturo, who seems to embrace the revolution, but Arturo ultimately betrays and is betrayed by the people around him. Galich again uses presentational devices to break the realism of the domestic drama, but he only breaks the realistic tone twice.

In the play, Arturo has organized a strike at the Fabri-Plast Company. When he negotiates the terms with the company lawyer, Cottone, at the rise of act 3, the scene freezes as he is confronted by his comrades. They help him to understand and to articulate the workers' position. Galich most harshly criticizes those who, like Arturo, become involved with people from the United States. Although Galich uses the play to deliver a scathing commentary about Guatemalans who benefit from the economic imperialism of the United States, he alludes to the coming revolution. In a scene in which Arturo justifies his actions, saying that he is a natural leader of the people and should be in charge, Eva responds that she feels sorry for the workers. Her sister Clara goes further:

> And not just the workers. The revolution [is destroyed] as well with that sort of people. They're the kind who will put an end to it. They are neither outside enemies, nor a reaction from within. That's what the people are for. They're the kind that destroy from within, eat away at it. They are filth.[5]

This play represents the first time that Galich introduces a character from the United States, Vittorio Cottone. The play also marks the first time that

Galich makes race an issue, as Cottone mentions that, while he is from the United States, he was born in Sicily. Arturo observes that Cottone is dark: "One would think that all the gringos were fair."[6] Galich's ideas about race and nationalism evolve and become far more complex in later plays.

Galich left Guatemala after the democratic government was toppled by the United States in 1954. Galich spent some time in Mexico and in Argentina (where he had lived as the Guatemalan ambassador) before settling in Cuba after the Cuban Revolution. He probably chose Cuba because of its leftist political climate and its vibrant theatrical community. Galich continued to write plays and to experiment with different forms, but he made one last return to the Natas family in *El último cargo* (*The Last Charge*) (1966).

In *El último cargo,* the children of Lolo have reached middle age, and Enrique, the child of Eva and Marcos, is a young man. Galich sets the action after the democratic government has fallen. Enrique has joined the rebellion and is at odds with his father, who holds some rank in the current dictatorial regime. Enrique leaves his home, saying that he will drop Marcos's name of López and resume the name of Natas. He also swears that he will expose the atrocities for which Marcos is responsible.

A fellow revolutionary, César, has proof of the atrocities in the form of a film, which shows a U.S. Green Beret under interrogation. The soldier recounts information about the ways the U.S. Marines train armies in Latin America as part of their counterinsurgency campaigns. His accounts of how they train armies to torture and mutilate civilians horrify the men, but they confirm that the Guatemalan government receives support from the CIA in its attack on the Guatemalan people. The Green Beret also makes reference to Vietnam, tying the Alliance for Progress programs directly to the war in Southeast Asia. Enrique takes the film and hides it in his car.

Enrique attempts to reconcile his uncle Arturo, who he believes is his protector, with his mother and his aunt before he leaves to join the guerrillas. At a party, Marcos hears that his troops have destroyed a column of guerrillas but is horrified to learn that Enrique might have been in the group. Enrique had escaped, however, and it turns out that Arturo is responsible for the deaths of the guerrillas and had tried to make sure Enrique was killed. Arturo also turns out to be a CIA agent. Enrique and the other guerrillas confront Arturo, but he is killed by a shot that mysteriously comes through the window.

In *El último cargo,* Galich uses more of the theatrical devices present in his earlier plays. When César is wrestling with his conscience, he is confronted by Clara, Enrique, Marcos, and Arturo, who act as his thoughts. Instead of showing the film that César has in his possession, Galich uses live actors to act out the scene depicted on the film.

Galich's other plays follow, more or less, the same paradigm. He set the first play that he wrote in the 1960s, *El pescado indigesto* (*Indigestible Fish*) (1961), in the Roman Republic. The play reads like a typical Roman comedy, complete with clever slaves and mistaken identity, but it attacks the contemporary relationship of business and the military. Galich writes in the introduction:

> *El pescado indigesto* doesn't pretend to interpret Roman history. Nor does it attempt to fit itself into that history. But it seemed unavoidable to place the play's action in Rome during the first century B.C. because that was when the poet Gaius Valerius Catullus wrote his ruthless satires of Caesar. Nor was it of interest to me in *El pescado indigesto* to weigh whether the vices the poet and other contemporaries attributed to the great general were true or not. The truth is that Catullus, having unleashed his poisonous rancor against Caesar— the causes for which aren't relevant here—has left us, without meaning to, one of his most severe axioms, a symbol valid for all time.[7]

Galich refers to his character Mamurra, the military supplier, "(that is to say the unscrupulous businesses), as being in a tight marriage with Caesar (that is the spirit of war and colonization)."[8] Through this allegory, Galich criticizes capitalism, the force that drives colonization and imperialism. *El pescado indigesto* is Galich's only play that uses historical allegory and is not specific in character and setting to Central America.

In 1964 Galich returned to domestic satire with *Entre cuatro paredes* (*Between Four Walls*) (1964). The title itself is a play on words as Paredes is both the family name and the word *walls*. In the comedy, Galich returns to the *costumbre* form, focusing on the hypocrisy of the middle class. *Entre cuatro Paredes* closely resembles *M'hijo el bachiller* in tone and in style. Rosaura Paredes, although she supposedly champions illegitimate children and belongs to a society dedicated to doing so, wastes no time in firing her unmarried maid when she discovers that the maid is pregnant. Her daughter Amalia, set to marry Antonio, a young man who has an illegitimate child, must also break her engagement. The comedy ends happily, of course, when it turns out that Paredes's son Gonzalo is the father of the maid's child and when it becomes known that Antonio has not abandoned the care of his son. In other words, the Paredes family supports issues only when it is convenient to do so.[9]

In 1966 Galich attacked the clergy in *Pascual Abah.* The play is set in the sixteenth century at the beginning of the colonial period. Calling the play a "farsa mágica," Galich incorporated the Quiché culture in an indictment against the relationship of the church with business and the military. The title character's name, Pascual Abah, literally means "sacrificial stone" and is synonymous with the site at Chichicastenango. Abah finds himself caught in the crossfire of the colonial conflict with the indigenous people. He makes a Christ-like return at the end to find his revenge.

El tren amarillo

Galich's most nationalist drama was, without a doubt, *El tren amarillo (The Yellow Train)* (1954). Although his *costumbres,* such as *M'hijo el bachiller* and *Papá Natas* use the middle class as an example for his social satire and policial allegory, his nationalist dramas were critical of the obstacles to nation building: foreign capitalists and Guatemalan parties that profited from foreign investment. *El tren amarillo* made a sharp departure from previous *costumbres,* Galich's own included. This departure grew out of Galich's own participation in a radical movement to redefine Guatemala through the new revolutionary culture.

Galich painted a picture of the Caribbean coast as a multiracial fellowship of Guatemalan people. Although his plays deal with the lives of the multiracial poor, Galich himself was a criollo who came from some privilege. *El tren amarillo* would likely have been staged in Guatemala City for a *ladino,* bourgeois audience; however, in 1954, before the play was finished, the U.S. government, in a move to protect United Fruit's interests, staged a coup that overthrew Arbenz's democratic government and installed another dictator. The coup derailed the emerging national culture and forced Galich and others into permanent exile. The play ultimately premiered in Mexico City in 1957, more a memorialization of the emerging national culture than a rehearsal of it.

The three acts of the play follow the protagonists, a group of planters, as they are caught in a web of exploitation by the character A. Tom Bomb. Bomb is a metaphorical representation of the United States and a "modern Mephistopheles," as Julio Babruskinas writes in the play's introduction.

Act 1 is set in the general store of Mariano Quinto, a Chinese merchant. The characters who come to drink, dance, and buy necessities there represent a broad spectrum of Caribbean Guatemalan society. The sailors who come to drink in the bar talk of traveling the Caribbean with the ship's holds open, a dangerous practice intended to keep the precious banana cargo from becoming overripe. The planters in the store toast to their good fortune and look forward to continuing good business with the schooners who come to buy their banana crop. This is before the diabolical plans of the company, here La Bananera, squeeze out the independent growers. Sensing this possible dark future, a planter recounts his bad experience with the company in Costa Rica. He also expresses his reservations about the coming railroad:

> *Bermúdez:* And so I say this of the trains . . . I may seem to be an enemy of progress. But there is progress and there is progress. . . .
>
> *Belisario:* . . . I don't understand how progress can crush a people.
>
> *Boesche:* I don't understand it either. Will it be that there is something like a great hidden clock, its machinery we can't even imagine?
>
> *Johnson:* And that the Devil winds, perhaps.
>
> *Bermúdez:* Could be. We only hear the bells, but without knowing where they are.[10]

Bermúdez's nightmare of the machinations of the devil seem to come true in the character of A. Tom Bomb, a Yankee imperialist who invades Guatemala. Bomb seems to manipulate the action from without. He controls the flashback of Bermúdez and intervenes often to change the course of events. At the end of act 1, after Bomb leaves for the capital to propose his idea for a railroad, everything takes a turn for the worse.

In acts 2 and 3, the stage is divided between the house of the company superintendent and the *yarda,* the collective dwelling of the workers on the plantation. Several years have passed since the action of act 1. Among the workers are the planters from act 1, who by now have been driven out of business by La Bananera and bought out. The stage directions direct that train whistles are heard from time to time in the background. They are the whistles of the banana trains as they speed the crop to the docks to be loaded onto ships bound for the United States.

Throughout the rest of the play, the oppression by the company worsens as company management seeks to crush the one last rival, a company called simply La Rival. With the help of Bomb, La Bananera tightens its hold on the government by installing its own choice for president, the illiterate police lieutenant from act 1. In exchange for this promotion, the newly installed president creates an extremely repressive government and extends the power of law enforcement to the officers of the company itself. By act 3, workers are found executed in the field for stealing bananas to eat.

For Galich, the map of the preimperialist nation looks like the general store of Mariano Quinto, the despised Chinese merchant. The store provides the site of important historical events that lead up to the revolution of 1944. It also provides a gathering place for a diverse cross-section of the Guatemalan population.

As Galich attempts to establish a people, he draws the boundary between insider and outsider along racial lines. In revolutionary Guatemala, the mobilization of the middle class added new racial variables to the political dialogue. The image of a racially diverse Guatemala circulated within cultural expressions against the now outdated image of Guatemala as a nation of elite criollos.

The setting of act 1 offers an image of the nation as racially diverse, as being made up of more than the dominant white criollo class; one planter is a criollo, one is black, and the other is mestizo. Although there is some discussion by the planters of racism being a problem in Guatemala, the general feeling among the Guatemalans seated at the table is that racial differences are unimportant: "Between us it doesn't make a difference," the mestizo planter says to the black planter.[11]

Galich presents a multiracial group of characters with which the audience is to identify as essentially Guatemalan. They would also recognize that which is not Guatemalan. Galich constructs the Chinese character, Mariano Quinto, and the character of A. Tom Bomb as the outsiders to provide a contrast to those who are recognizable as Guatemalan. Bomb, the Yankee imperialist, represents the economic exploitation by a U.S. company; instead of trying to accomplish this contrast with the Yankee imperialist alone, Galich used the local storeowner. The imperialist represents an adversary too powerful and too absent to be entirely effective in this role. Mariano, who represents Chinese laborers imported by the United States, provides an easier target of anti-imperialist resentment.

Within the exchanges in the store, Mariano displays undesirable characteristics. He is drawn against, and preys upon, the "true" Guatemalans around him who are good and noble enough to bear his abuse. He forces Hortensia, who works in the store, into prostitution against her will. She must sleep with the sailors who drink in the bar or lose her job.

Mariano acts only to serve his own interests. When trouble breaks out in the form of fighting among the sailors, he hides behind his counter and blows the police whistle. When the Yankee imperialist A. Tom Bomb appears, Mariano offers no information beyond what he can sell:

> *Bomb:* I want to continue my journey to the capital of the country. How can I get there?
>
> *Mariano:* (*With a heavy, comical Chinese "accent."*) Onry by mule.
>
> *Bomb:* And how far is it?
>
> *Mariano:* I don't know. Perhaps a hundred reagues. Mister, would you rike someting?
>
> *Bomb:* No, thanks. I want to head out to the capital today. How can I get mules?
>
> *Mariano:* Ah, not possible, not possible.
>
> *Bomb:* (*Smiling.*) I pay in Dollars.
>
> *Mariano:* So, entirery easy.[12]

Primarily, the scene reveals Mariano's greed and laziness. He remains conveniently ignorant until a U.S. dollar is offered as payment. Then he gladly offers his help. On another level, Mariano acts out the perceived relationship between the Chinese merchants and the U.S. banks. His subservience to the dollar represents Chinese labor originally hired by United Fruit to build the railroads in Central America. The scene underscores the relationship of the two foreigners.

Mariano cheats a desperate woman with a very sick child. The woman, Matilda, brings in her boy, who she reports cannot eat or keep anything down. Mariano looks him over and announces that the child has tapeworm and that Matilda can buy the medicine for two *reales*. Matilda cannot afford it, at which point a generous Belisario, a planter, offers to pay for the treatment. As Matilda leaves with the medicine, Belisario, noting the boy's jaundice, expresses doubts about Mariano's diagnosis:

> *Belisario:* I think that doesn't add up. Are you sure that he had worms?
>
> *Mariano:* Sure. Here all have worm, all have bloated berry, all yerrow of jaundice. Now who knows what is my yerrow of Chinese and what is my yerrow of jaundice.
>
> *Belisario:* That isn't an explanation to say that the child had worms.
>
> *Mariano:* It couldn't be other irrness.
>
> *Belisario:* And why not?
>
> *Mariano:* Because I don't have other medicine.[13]

The statement "Because I don't have other medicine" demonstrates that Mariano is either stupid or completely immoral. His diagnosis fits whatever he has for sale and does nothing to help the sick child. He also charges a high price as indicated by Matilda's inability to pay. In contrast, the Guatemalan shows his concern and pays for her medicine.

In the same scene, the audience discovers that people such as Matilda are an easy target for unscrupulous businesspeople such as Mariano. He operates the only business in the small port town, and the railroad does not reach that part of the country. Matilda tells Belisario that she cannot go to a doctor because there is no doctor within traveling distance. She says that Mariano is her only option. In the historical moment of the story, the characters speak with hope of the train that will rectify the problem, but the audience knows that the transportation monopoly of United Fruit, the very railroad that promises to create possibility, will crush the very people who harbor that hope. Matilda's diseased child stands out as a victim of both the jaundice that makes him yellow and the storeowner who cheats his mother.

The second layer of victimization becomes visible because the audience may associate the Chinese with the workers imported from the United States to build the railroads. The visible presence of the Chinese collapses into the invisible presence of the United States and becomes a clear target of anti-imperialist hatred. In this moment the "yerrow of Chinese" and the "yerrow of jaundice" become one and the same.

The ethereal nature of the U.S. character, Bomb, resists being stereotyped. Bomb ominously narrates from the side of the action and illustrates, through enacted flashback scenes, the evils that the United States has visited upon the countries of Central America. When the planters discuss their current troubles with the United Fruit Company, Bomb tells the audience about the long history of his relationship with the Central American region. He enacts a flashback scene with young Bermúdez, then a planter in Costa Rica. The company refused the crop that Bermúdez brought to the docks because he had refused to sign a ten-year contract.[14] Bomb acts as the mechanism that shows the audience this scene from the planter's past and creates the link that demonstrates the length and scope of the company's domination in the region.

The cunning and deceitful nature of Bomb reads as a symbol of the then-recent imperialist exploitation and lacks the psychological depth of characters who represent "real" people. Lights change when Bomb enters and exits the stage, and he moves, often unnoticed by the other characters, when he does cross into the stage action. He represents rather than embodies.

The two characters, Bomb and Mariano, work together to establish a clear boundary. The audience may identify the source of imperialist evil in the figure of Bomb, but it may also draw a tighter circle in opposition to the easily recognizable Chinese foreigner. The group defined against these two figures makes up the Guatemalan people, the hardworking multiracial planters who possess essentially Guatemalan characteristics, such as generosity and a strong sense of fairness. With the configuration of the Guatemalan people agreed upon, Galich can then demonstrate how the Guatemalan national character survives the pressure of imperialist domination.

The presence of Yankee landowners creates many situations that demonstrate the Guatemalan character reacting to pressures from a foreign invasion. Situations arise that highlight the durability and strength of the Guatemalan identity, but they also create its sense of realness. The movement of the plot through this history also creates the sense of the continuity of identity.

The train provides one such example of Guatemalans reacting to the foreign invasion. In act 1 the characters acknowledge that little transportation exists on the Caribbean coast. At one point, the development of the railroad seems like a great help to people with little resources, such as Matilda, who cannot find adequate medical attention for her sick child. However, in act 2, the ever-present banana trains cannot carry a dying planter. The Guatemalans seem better off without the constant reminder of the train whistle as it carries off their livelihood but cannot save their lives.

When the Guatemalans can no longer function at the hands of the foreigners, they must counter foreign labels for their ideas and their actions. Galich presents a scene in which the U.S. company managers call the workers Communists and ask whether they are on strike:

Mr. Whip: You are Communists.

Canche: (*With humor not void of sympathy.*) But Mister Whip, we scarcely have time to rest. No one here has seen a book, nor a newspaper, or anything, nor has anyone heard of anyone who speaks of these things you say. It is much more simple. It is hunger and desperation. We thought that you would hear us on this, but since that isn't so, the trains aren't going to move.

Mr. Whip: That is a strike.

Canche: I don't know what it is called. Perhaps it is a strike.[15]

The foreign supervisor attempts to apply labels to the actions of the Guatemalan workers. However, the terms *Communist* and *strike* seem artificial against a completely natural reflex to stop working because of weakness brought on by starvation.

The character of the Guatemalans is essential and unchanging in the three acts of the play; their values and convictions are made stronger by the conflict with the corrupt managers of La Bananera. Galich effectively creates a multiracial people and binds them together in opposition to the U.S. and Chinese "invasion." He heightens this effect by creating a situation in which the invader questions the multiracial composition of Guatemalan peoplehood. In act 2, company goons attack the black planter, Johnson. As he lies dying in the workers' housing, his comrades work quickly to find a way to transport him to a doctor. The trains cannot carry him to a doctor because they are full of cargo. The train he can take will not arrive for hours and will take even longer to transport him over the mountains. Meanwhile, the management will not allow for the use of the motorcar: "You are crazy. How could a black man ride in the motorcar of the Superintendent?"[16] The superintendent goes on to quote the law in Alabama. Racism in Galich's drama is an importation of U.S. ideology, and its invocation here creates a clear boundary between the Guatemalans, who have agreed that race does not matter, and the Other, who invokes racist laws. But Galich's most interesting problemization of race is embodied in the character of Canche.

Canche means "blond" in the local slang of the Caribbean coast of Guatemala. As a child, Canche grows up in the *yarda* of the workers of the La Bananera plantation. He has no idea that his father, the despised gringo superintendent, Mr. Whip, makes his living on the backs of the workers Canche leads in the workers' revolt.

Hortensia had met Canche's gringo father, Mr. Whip, or "Joe," when he was a sailor drinking in Mariano's bar. He danced with her often and told her his dreams. They imagined a life together in which he would own his own schooner and they would make money transporting bananas themselves. When a fight broke out between Joe and the other sailors, Joe missed his boat because the others beat him senseless. Joe expressed disappointment at missing his boat, but Hortensia assured him that he would still find a way to accomplish his dream. The planters generously offer land that he could farm:

> *Belisario:* He can become a good banana planter, isn't that true, gentlemen?
> *Boesche:* There is land for all. Why not? The only thing you need to do is work.

Johnson: I say the same. I have little, but I offer it to you.

Hortensia: God bless you. He will pay you well, Don Belisario. I know how to work and nothing scares me, because I have done it. Do you hear that, Joe? We will be able to buy the schooner. (*Joe nods yes.*)

Johnson: That's a lot, Miss. But the work can give you that and much more. . . . If you are lucky.

Belisario: Time will tell. (*To the others.*) This guy needs to rest. But where should we take him?

Hortensia: To my room. . . . (*The planters look at each other.*) It's always been this way when he has come here . . . for something very different than you would imagine.

Belisario: Yes, I know. We are simple, like this love of yours. We know about the hard things in life, but we respect the great things that it has.

Boesche: Yes, it is true. More sacred than the pretenses of uprightness that I have known.

Hortensia: From now on, it will be his home. And nothing more. I swear to you, that no one else made it so. God must have meant for it to be this way.

Johnson: This is very noble. Well said. It is the will of God. He knows how to create a pure home, where before it had been a swamp.[17]

Hortensia's former life as a prostitute doesn't matter to these gentlemen, who understand that she worked in order to survive. The men believe that her discovery of such divine love redeems her. They generously give her and the sailor, a stranger to them, offers of land to help them get started in their new lives.

Even Mariano, usually greedy, knows that he cannot stand in the way of her happiness when he says: "Go. Maliano knows you never leturn. Now you had mallied and tomollow baby. No good you work Maliano Quinto's house. But I content if you find happiness and are good woman. Go, go."[18] The audience will see the baby to which he alludes in the next act as the fully grown, blond, and fair Canche.

Twenty years later, in the *yarda* of La Bananera, Joe Whip does not even remember Hortensia and has no idea that the man who incites the other workers to strike is his own son. As superintendent of the company, Joe Whip must find the ringleader of the unrest and have him eliminated. Bad omens surround his final showdown with the young man: Hortensia and Belisario hear a train whistle when there should be no train, and Belisario suddenly thinks of "los hijos de agua" (the children of water), which are the buds of the banana bushes that are cut if they reappear.

When the other workers see Canche together with Joe Whip, they ominously remark at their similarities.

Acting out his duties, Joe makes a phone call to have Canche detained and assassinated by the government police, which, by this act, are under company control. Hortensia, reading the bad signs she encounters after Canche leaves her, finds Joe and tells him that Canche is their son. The realization makes Joe change his mind. He has a chance to change what will happen to Canche, to stop the train that will carry Canche to the capital and into government hands, and he begins to ring up the men who will take his life. An intervention by Bomb stops Joe by convincing him that the company sacrifices its own children in order to keep the trains running.

Canche symbolizes an invasion of Guatemala by imperialism. He was conceived by the false promises of a sailor (the United States) to a destitute woman (Guatemala). Galich creates a complicated character who becomes a martyr of the anti-imperialist movement. Hortensia hopes that the mutual blood flowing in Canche's veins will save him, as well as the people of Guatemala. However, Canche gets in the way of the company's agenda, and the superintendent would sooner sacrifice his own flesh before allowing the profits of the company to slow down.

This tale of the multiracial fellowship that is Guatemala and its struggle against foreign imperialism seems unfinished in that it ends before the popular revolution of 1944. The picture the play paints is a dark one, with the hybrid national culture that was conceived from imperialism about to be wiped away from the Guatemalan landscape. Perhaps Galich had intended to return to the men of the company and to the family of Joe, Hortensia, and Canche in the way that he followed the Natas family. Regardless, since he wrote the play at the height of the revolutionary regime, he must have known that the rhetorical element of the play would enable the national audience to fill in the blank at the end. The citizen would know that this fellowship ultimately triumphed. Unfortunately, Galich and the others discovered, before the curtain could rise on the play, that the triumph was short-lived.

In his exile, Galich spent some time reworking his major works and writing plays for children. He compiled a book of dramas for children while he was in Cuba, called *Teatrinos* (*Little Plays*) (1983). Galich taught courses in literature and history at the Universidad de La Habana. He was also the director of the department of theatre of the Casa de las Américas. This entailed acting as editor of the theatre magazine *Conjunto,* which he founded in 1964, and organizing the annual theatre festivals. He served in this position until his death. Galich also edited several books for the Casa de las Américas on historical figures such as Simón Bolívar and Benito Juárez. Manuel Galich died on August 30, 1984. He is buried in the Cementerio Colón in Havana, Cuba.

5 EUROPEAN THOUGHT AND INDIGENOUS DREAMS

The mestizo characters in nationalist drama create a particular vision of a people in four ways. First, they create a cohesive sense of a national race by using the image of the mixed white and indigenous person as the national symbol. Second, they provide a tie between the people of a nation and their original roots, making it natural that the people feel patriotic about their "native" land. Third, they represent a set of characteristics that are thought to be typical of each of the nation's citizens by employing characteristics from stereotypes of European and indigenous people. Fourth, the appropriation of the indigenous people as a national symbol is also often an appropriation of the indigenous struggle against colonialism.

The Nicaraguan national anthem used during the Sandinista regime speaks of a people who are fed by the blessed "sangre de Diriangén," the blood of an indigenous hero. The Nicaraguan people in the song, which was sung at all important national events, are imagined as a race of people. This image is performed again and again, yet all the singers are not necessarily mestizo, let alone indigenous.

It is not important that all of the anthem's singers truly have indigenous blood in their veins. It is important that all the singers visualize themselves as a cohesive and continuous culture and that they see themselves as the natural culture. By identifying themselves as "indigenous," the citizens imagine their culture as the essential culture of Nicaragua— a nation that did not exist, per se, before colonization but that was waiting for the Nicaraguan people to advance and to liberate it.

Similarly, in Alan Bolt's *Banana Republic*, the character Sandino delivers a modified quote from the real Sandino's writings:

We are nationalists and we are proud that we have indigenous American blood flowing through our veins, noble and generous blood.[1]

Sandino actually wrote:

I am Nicaraguan and I feel proud because Indian blood, above all, flows in my veins, which carries the mystery of being a loyal and sincere patriot.[2]

Sandino used the first person to explain, in his first manifesto, his reasons for not laying down his arms when others of the Liberal Party gave in to pressure from the United States. Bolt extended the sentiment to all Nicaraguans and tied it to a particularly nationalist ideology. Sandino's 1927 quote belies some notions about possessing indigenous blood, which gives this patriotism a mystic and spiritual quality.

The Nicaraguan Pablo Antonio Cuadra does not explicitly identify the race of the protagonist Sebastiano. He does, however, describe Sebastiano's wife, Juana, in the cast list of *Por los caminos van los campesinos* as specifically mestiza. The description reads: "Mestiza; imaginative. More of a dreamer. With birds in the head, but ingenuous and true. Talkative and optimistic."[3] Cuadra presents Juana in contrast to her husband Sebastiano, not identified as mestizo and so presumably criollo, whom Cuadra describes as "frank," "thoughtful," and "fatalistic."[4] Cuadra expresses the dichotomy of the practical criollo versus the dreamy native in an interview cited by Randy Martin.[5] Cuadra speaks of the fusion of European and indigenous cultures:

The Greco-Roman tradition is more accessible through our language: by speaking Spanish we keep speaking Greek and Latin. The indigenous is more difficult because it has scarcely been expressed in language and what there is becomes a challenge. But this challenge, I believe, inspires creativity and opens mysterious zones of human thought and feeling that the western world, with its excess of rationalism, has forgotten.[6]

Martin asserts that Cuadra sees the mestizo as a "synthesis achieved through the fusion of European rationality and indigenous mystery."[7] Cuadra calls for the incorporation of both cultures into the national cultural project, celebrating both the original culture of Nicaragua and the European civilizing force.

The dichotomy of the rationality of the thoughtful and the irrationality of the dreamer surfaces in other Nicaraguan dramas as well, where the combination of the two works in favor of the Nicaraguans defending their homeland. In *La niña del río* (*Child of the River*) (1943), Enrique Fernández Morales creates a heroine who embodies this dichotomy.

Rafaela de Herrera y Uriarte, famous in Nicaraguan history for defending the mouth of the San Juan River against the British in 1762, comes from a mixed family. Her mother, the mestiza, had died some time before the action of the play, and her father, the Spanish general José de Herrera, lays dying at the start of the play. The indigenous blood in Rafaela's veins could be her undoing as she sadly sits by the river, unable to do anything but stare into the water and listen to the sounds of the jungle. A trusted old soldier of the general comes out to the riverbank to bid her to come inside, and she refuses:

> Bartolo: . . . You are exactly like your mother; sweet, sad and as impassioned as she. Only love draws you out of your shyness.
>
> Rafaela: (*Leaning on the tree, as if to protect herself, speaking low*). It is the sadness of the Indians. We carry it in our blood like a heritage that is both precious and evil at once. My mother was mestiza. My father said that he never got used to her silence and aloofness. We Indians are sad, Bartolo, with a resigned and high sadness. Also the River is sad and mysterious and impenetrable. I understand it and I love it because I am like it.
>
> Bartolo: Child! Don't get carried away with these oversentimentalities, which will end in illness; and don't forget that the Conquistadores call [the river] the Desaguadero, the Arm of Glory; and that you are Spanish with the clean blood of the nobility, the soldiers, and ancient Christians.[8]

Rafaela's indigenous blood gives her a connection to the river, which gives her an edge in the battle against the British. But it also paralyzes her as she gazes dreamily into the river as the invaders approach. The entire conflict of the play revolves around how to awaken the rational Spaniard in Rafaela so that she may lead the people of the castle against the British forces. Ultimately, her Spanish side wins her over, thankfully for those who need her protection. Rafaela must balance the part of her that is mystical and tied to the earth on the one hand and rational and coura- · geous on the other hand. Here the good qualities of both indigenous and Spanish blood meet in the ideal Nicaraguan. Although the combination of her heritage had the potential to immobilize Rafaela, the European blood tamed the wild indigenous spirit in the end.

Rafaela's Spanish awakening comes from deep inside her, like a latent set of characteristics triggered by necessity. Her father dies before he can give orders for the battle against the British, and no one else feels capable to lead, being natural followers, as Bartolo points out: "How am I going to help [Rafaela] in that, Sebastiana. I am only a soldier and I know how to obey when I am ordered, but thinking has never been my strong point."[9] As the canoes of the pirates enter the San Juan River, a strange and mystical change comes over Rafaela:

> What is required of a maid in as hard a situation? (*Pause*) I feel a new warmth moving inside my muscles; I feel a call in my chest that animates me and gives me courage. I feel forces which order me in gesture and voice: impulses inside my blood which compel my decision.... [N]ow in this Castle no one gives orders but me![10]

As naturally as she feels a connection to the river, Rafaela also naturally leads the Spanish soldiers to victory. Because of her highborn lineage, she cannot help but to rally even as the odds are against them. For Rafaela, giving up the castle to the heretical British means giving them "my honor, my lineage, my love, and the honor of my nation,"[11] and because of her noble nature, she does not have the capacity to surrender those things.

As Friar Francisco gives the benediction over the dead of both sides of the battle, he casts a wider circle to include more than the mestizos in the makeup of the Nicaraguan people:

> [T]hat a special providence is granted, the dispossessed men of distant races, negroes, British, Indians, zambos,[12] mestizos, mulattoes[,] and Spaniards, fertilize the heart of this noble land, so that within her grows the tree of peace, of Indulgence, of the brotherhood of the coexistence of lineages, of the eternal and infinite prosperity that is the basis of the law and justice of Christ.[13]

Where the mestiza character creates the dual benefit of one tied to the land and tied to God, the benediction unites the diverse people of Nicaragua under the divine right to the land, initialized by the mestiza.

Guatemala and the Mayans

References to a nation's indigenous people function as representations of the struggle against foreign domination. In Guatemala, the renaissance of indigenous culture at the beginning of the twentieth century grew as much out of a reaction to U.S. imperialism as out of a reaction against the oppression of indigenous people. Eduardo Galeano, fighting with Guatemalan rebels against U.S.-backed forces, also invokes the image of the indigenous people as a symbol of the anti-imperialist struggle. In a chapter of his book *Guatemala* that he opens with a quote from the Popul Vuh, Galeano says:

> The Indians' attitude will be the decisive attitude in the Guatemalan rev-
> olution. What will be their response to the challenge of the battle that is al-
> ready being fought in their name and that of all exploited Guatemalans? Will
> they recognize their own lost voice in the protest that is being expressed with
> bullets?[14]

Galeano identifies with indigenous people who have lost their land to colonial invasion.

With Guatemala's 1944 revolution came a greater interest in indigenous culture and the establishment of the Indigenous Institute, an organization devoted to the study of Guatemala's indigenous people. The
first of the Guatemalan theatrical works using Mayan mythology, Manuel
Galich's *El señor Gukup-Cakix* (*Mr. Gukup-Cakix*) (1939), follows the
story from the Popul Vuh of Gukup Cakix's encounter with the hero
twins Xbalanqué and Hunahpu. Gukup Cakix was an arrogant giant who
felt that his existence made the sun and the moon obsolete. His sons spent
their time making earthquakes; this, combined with Gukup Cakix's ar-
rogance, was more than the twins could take. The hero twins attempted
to destroy Gukup while he was eating fruit from his favorite tree. They
caused him to fall, injuring his jaw and loosening his teeth, but he tore
off one of the twins' arms in his anger.

The twins were aided by their parents, who disguised themselves and
entered the home of Gukup and his wife, Chimalmat. They fooled Gukup
into believing that they could fix his aching teeth. They removed all of them
and replaced them with grains of corn, thereby robbing him of his power.
They also blinded him by removing his eyes. With Gukup's teeth and eyes
removed, the twins easily defeated him and retrieved the missing arm.

Galich was but one of several literary figures to use Mayan culture and
mythology. The man most famous for his literary use of the Mayan culture is Nobel laureate Miguel Ángel Asturias (1899–1974). Asturias wrote
two plays based on his study at the Sorbonne of indigenous language and
culture. Although *Audencia de los confines* (*Governorship of the Frontier*)
(1957) more directly attacks government policies toward indigenous Guatemalans, *Soluna* (*Sunmoon*) (1955) is an aesthetically more interesting
work, and it has received greater acclaim and attention. This difference
may have resulted because of the years in which the plays were written.
Audencia de los confines came just after the coup that overthrew the demo-

cratic government and focuses on the social aspects of *mestizaje*. By 1957 more oppressive policies were in place against indigenous people, which sparked Asturias to write a more scathing critique of those policies, which were part of a U.S.-backed war against Communist insurrection. George McMurray suggests in *Spanish American Writing since 1941* that, although Bartolomé de las Casas perseveres over his opponents in the play, Asturias alludes to the continued persecution of indigenous people in modern Guatemala.[15] However, the critique remains cloaked behind the historical theme. Both of these plays, and Asturias's other literary work, have caused many Guatemalans to look to Asturias as a voice for the indigenous people during the twentieth century.

Miguel Ángel Asturias as a Voice for the Indigenous

Miguel Ángel Asturias grew up in Guatemala and earned a law degree at the University of San Carlos. He showed interest in the indigenous people of Guatemala even then when he wrote his thesis, *El problema social del indio* (*The Social Problem of the Indian*) (1923). But Asturias did not pursue this interest until he studied at the Sorbonne.

Asturias had meant to study political economy in England, but he stayed only for a few months there before heading to Paris. After he attended lectures by Georges Raynaud on the Mayans, he decided to study with Raynaud, and he remained in Paris for ten years. Asturias studied and helped translate the Popol Vuh and wrote a book on Mayan myth, *Leyendas de Guatemala* (*Legends of Guatemala*), in 1930.

No doubt, exposure to the avant-garde writers and artists of the time influenced much of Asturias's writing. Asturias is probably best known for his novel *El Señor Presidente* (*Mr. President*), which he wrote during his time abroad. The novel reflects the growing paranoia of the time of his childhood, when Manuel Estrada Cabrera was dictator. According to McMurray, the scenes in the novel reflect Asturias's familiarity with surrealism and expressionism, with hallucinations, dreamlike sequences, and the characters' distorted sense of time and distance. McMurray points to one scene in particular in which the wife of a condemned man rushes to the prison to try to stop her husband's execution. In her anxiety, she imagines that the wheels of her coach have stopped turning, leaving her suspended, unable to reach him.[16] Each character must in some way reconcile reality with the distorted reality of living under such terror.

The book could not be published during the Ubico regime, the government to which Asturias returned when he came back to Guatemala in 1933. It was not until 1946 that the book was published, after the fall of Ubico, during the democratic government of Arévalo. Arévalo appointed Asturias as cultural attaché to the Guatemalan embassy in Mexico, which is where the book was first published. The following year, Asturias went to Argentina as cultural attaché to the embassy there.

When Asturias returned from Argentina in 1948, he finished writing one of his most intriguing books, *Hombres de maíz* (*Men of Maize*), published the following year. Although this marks a return to his study of indigenous culture, several scholars have pointed out the continuation of surrealist influences[17]; Asturias felt differently:

> Surrealism was perhaps too intellectual; . . . ours, that of the primitive mentality relating to the indigenous world, we have this aspect of a subterranean, submagical world, more directly, not as an intellectual product, but rather . . . natural. We and the indigenous have generally two realities; a palpable reality and a dream reality.[18]

Asturias believed that the dreamlike qualities in this work are less surrealist and spring more from the indigenous culture itself. Regardless, the Mayan dream world and the mythological themes would resurface again in other novels and in his dramatic works.

Hombres de maíz follows the Quiché Mayans of Guatemala through the final encroachment of European culture, assimilation and genocide, and the hopeful images of future resurgence and resistance. Two of the book's most prominent Mayan themes, that of the *tecunas* or "spider-stung" women, and that of the *nagual,* or the animal counterpart, also appear as strong themes in Asturias's first play, *Soluna,* in 1955. The *tecunas* are reflected in the name of Asturias's character María Tecún, a woman who ate *piñole* (ground, roasted corn) through which spiders had crawled. Therefore, like the *tecunas* of legend, she was cursed to flee her husband and her home and to be eternally pursued by her husband. Finally, Tecún turns to stone.[19] Critics were both baffled and impressed with the disjointed nature of the book, for which Asturias offered no apologies. According to Gerald Martin, Asturias said: "there are no concessions. There is no plot. Things may be clear or not. They are just there."[20]

As did Galich, Asturias wrote about the imperialism of the United Fruit Company in a trilogy of novels. The first of these, *Viento fuerte* (*Strong Wind*), appeared in 1950. The other two of the "*bananera* trilogy," *El Papa verde* (*The Green Pope*) and *Los ojos de los enterrados* (*Eyes of the Interred*) appeared in 1954 and 1960, respectively. He also wrote angrily of the 1954 overthrow of the democratic regime in *Week-end in Guatemala,* 1956. Asturias also wrote his first stage play, *Soluna,* during this time.

The Marriage of the Sun and the Moon in *Soluna*

> *Mauro:* I want to believe! Do you know what [it] means for me to want to
> believe in the Chama Soluna, and not be able to believe?
> —Miguel Ángel Asturias, *Soluna*

Soluna provides a window into Asturias's problematic relationship with his indigenous subject. Asturias uses Mayan imagery and mythology with affection, portraying his Mayan characters sympathetically. The text is rich with characters who repeat the mixed indigenous and criollo folklore of the countryside. But the structure of *Soluna* betrays Asturias, revealing his deep ambiguity about the role of the Mayans in Guatemalan culture and his own relationship to that culture. It also reveals the ambiguity with which native Guatemalans view Asturias.

The cycle of *Soluna* takes us through the departure and return of Ninica, a city girl married to a rural *patrón,* Mauro. Her departure is frantic, almost catastrophic, with Mauro attempting to slow her down with claims of being unable to find his hat. Ninica rushes out of the door to catch the train that will speed her back to the capital, with Mauro attempting to head her off while the sky opens up with a torrential downpour.

Porfirión and Tomasa, the hired help, spend the next scene describing the departure and musing about their parts in the attempt to stall Ninica. They note how the couple's affection for one another mirrors that of cats in heat; Ninica calls him "Mau," and Mauro calls her "mi animalito" (my little animal). The first references to Mayan mythology creep into the dialogue as the characters contemplate what type of tree they might be in the next life.

At this point we see the difference between the superstitious but largely Catholic views of Tomasa and the mostly Mayan worldview of Porfirión when Tomasa declares, "What does a tree have to do with burying a Christian?"[21] When Porfirión states that his departed friend Rumauldo wanted to be a cedar, Tomasa replies, "We are going to be a bag of worms and you are choosing your smell!"[22] When a group of oxen drivers arrive, they speak of Chama Soluna, the mysterious seer who speaks in riddle. The Chama Soluna is at once the source of fear and desire; the people of the area seek his advice but become fearful when they cannot make sense of it. But what is more curious to the local people is that someone has recently spotted the horse of the *patrón* outside of the Chama's place, an indication that the rational Mauro has also sought the Chama's counsel.

A group of gypsies arrive at the house. Asturias uses colorful language and humor as the old couple and their daughter sing of the pots and pans they have for sale, their transient lives, and allusions to things that might happen in the future. They also have some prophetic abilities, but the servants disdain them as thieves. The gypsies tell the servants that Ninica will return that night. The gypsy woman reads her cards and tells them that Ninica "goes on a trip, but does not leave," and "she leaves in the train, but she is going to have supper here."[23] Tomasa and Porfirión express skepticism because Ninica could not return so quickly unless the *patrón* convinced her to stay. Then Porfirión believes the gypsy when she attributes this to an impending eclipse: "(the gypsy rises and moves from side to side saying) The eclipse! The eclipse! Sun and moon will make contact! And then they will end the pact!"[24] Although the servants do not know of any pact, the image of the eclipse makes sense to them. The title *Soluna* alludes to both the name of the seer, Chama Soluna, and the event of the eclipse, Sol y luna, Sun and Moon. Profirión shudders when the gypsies leave and tells Tomasa that he worries that his *nagual*, his animal spirit, will surface during the eclipse. Indeed, while Tomasa goes to get a candle to light the darkening room, the figure of Porfirión shifts into a black coyote and howls at the mask hanging over the fireplace. When Tomasa returns, the coyote disappears and Porfirión is himself again.

Tomasa decides that they should dispose of the mask, which to her represents witchcraft. But Porfirión will not touch the mask, which was given to Mauro by the Chama Soluna. Tomasa tries to reach it herself, causing Porfirión to panic:

> Do not touch it, Mrs. Tomasa! (*Lets go of the chair that he had held firmly and retreats.*) Do not touch it! Do not touch it. . . . It is the mask of the eclipses . . . , the mask of the Chama Soluna, half sun and half moon, the one that causes time to run, that makes years pass in a minute and centuries in a day. . . .[25]

Tomasa removes the mask because she believes that the principal place in a house, over the fireplace, should be reserved for Catholic icons.

Mauro's return in the second act marks the beginning of the prophesies that come to pass. Mauro asks for Ninica's place setting to be put on the table with his own. Tomasa tells Mauro that he should not trust

Porfirión in part because of his *nagual*. She trusts the person, but not the animal. She also suggests that Ninica is a *tecuna:*

> For that reason we shouldn't let little girls eat dirt when they are young, because if, by accident, they eat dirt walked on by a spider, they seal a pact that makes them always flee from the ones they love, and poor women, they are not to blame. Who can blame Doña Ninica? I spied on her. Sometimes she moved almost without touching the ground, lighter than air, and sometimes she collapsed and became like a stone. I have everything, she said, but I need something! She is a Tecuna, someone who has everything but is never satisfied. And my fear is that you are going to go after her, looking for her, following her, just as I saw you today.[26]

Ninica is like the women of *Hombres de maíz*, always fleeing their husbands who follow behind, pursuing them.

Tomasa also warns Mauro about visiting the Chama Soluna, but Mauro does not take stock in the rumors about the seer. He asks for the mask of Chama Soluna to be rehung. Mauro's casual view of the Chama belies an even bigger gap of belief, because Mauro longs to share the cosmology of the people around him. When he and Porfirión share a drink and discuss the Chama Soluna, the gap between rational thought and belief becomes clear:

> *Mauro:* Well for me, much to your dismay, the Chama Soluna is a man like all the others. . . .
> *Porfirión:* No, *patrón,* he is a seer!
> *Mauro:* I know, I am not going to deny that he knows the curative power of certain herbs . . .
> *Porfirión:* He is a seer, not because he knows! He is a seer because he divines!
> *Mauro:* Yes, that's what people say. Who is going to deny that he is a man who knows the order in which the stars turn, the natural laws that the wind and the rain, and the hail obey, . . .
> *Porfirión:* No, sir, pardon me for contradicting you, I may seem rude, but that's not the case! The Chama Soluna was given sight at birth. It is like the stones that glow at night.[27]

Mauro can't see Chama Soluna as anything more than a man with knowledge about the natural world. The idea that Soluna is touched with anything more does not fit with Mauro's rational worldview.

While Mauro does not understand, he covets the beliefs of Porfirión and the others. Porfirión explains his animal counterpart, telling Mauro that a person cannot live without it. When Mauro asks if that means the person dies, Porfirión explains that the person is neither living nor dead, but that the individual goes through life without a life force. Mauro breaks:

> Then I want to believe. To believe in the Chama. To have my life force. I want to believe, Porfirión! I want to believe! Do you know what it means for me to want to believe in the Chama Soluna, and not be able to believe? Not be able to believe that that mask makes time run! Not be able to believe and to want to believe that that mask turns the days in minutes and the years in hours. . . . I want to believe. I want to believe. (*Forgetting Porfirión, shouts from the door towards the night.*) I want to believe!![28]

This outburst frightens Porfirión until Mauro laughs at himself and blames the liquor that the two men have been drinking. After Porfirión leaves, Mauro continues his lament over not sharing the beliefs of the people around him:

> I want to believe, to believe as these people believe, like Porfirión, like Tomasa, with the faith of the late Rumualdo, with the faith of the midwife Venustiana, as the ox drivers believe. (*Smokes deeply.*) Yes, yes, I would trade places with anyone of them, with such a great contented feeling of children and their faith. No other faith. Their faith. Their faith! Life, mother, warmth. (*Smokes.*) Yes, if I could change places with anyone of them, if I only could, for the danger, the *nagual;* for the impossible, the miracle; for the hope, the mask of the Chama Soluna. Ah, to believe. To believe in the *nagual,* to believe in the miracle. To believe in the mask that tears time to pieces.[29]

Everyone around him shares the Mayan beliefs. Mauro envies them because this world is out of his reach.

Later, Mauro falls asleep in the armchair with the mask in his hand. The animal spirit, the *nagual,* of Porfirión enters and tries to pull the mask away from him. It hides when Mauro stirs, and it peers out at him when he rises and puts on the mask, causing the light on the stage to change. *Campesinos* enter the stage and begin a dance to symbolize the clash between the sun and the moon.

After the dance, some of the peasants appeal to Mauro, fearful that the end of the world has come. They implore with even greater urgency when the earth trembles. Several peasants kiss the ground and ask for mercy from the earth. After a brief comic exchange between them, all the peasants believe they hear someone coming, and they brace themselves for the end.

In a comic twist, the approaching footsteps are only those of the gyp-sies from the earlier scene. The peasants reason that it could not be the end of the world if the gypsies were still permitted to walk the earth. In fact, the peasants direct further wrath at the gypsies when they hear of the misfortune of the ox drivers who have lost three yokes of oxen, a new bell, and a horse over a cliff during the earthquake. Blaming the fortune-telling of the old gypsy woman, the peasants prepare to chase after them.

They are halted by the appearance in the doorway of Ninica, who seems mystified at arriving at her home: "But I was just . . . (*the suitcase is seen in her gloved hand*) Today I was just . . . It cannot be . . . Only I must have dreamed it . . . I went away, I arrived at the capital, I returned and it's still today."[30] Mauro offers wine to all in celebration of his wife's return. He raises his glass, drinks to the Chama Soluna, and offers his wishes that the mask help other people who are waiting for the arrival of some distant day, for freedom from prison, for a cure for illness, or to return home after being homesick abroad.

The light changes, and the peasants and Ninica disappear. Tomasa's scream at seeing Porfirión's animal spirit awakens Mauro, who was sleep-ing in the armchair. The animal spirit grabs the mask and runs. Mauro wakes up and loads his gun and shoots what he believes is a coyote.

The peasants arrive to tell Mauro that the train has derailed and many people are injured, including Ninica. They have come to prepare her bed and to bring her home to recover. Ninica has returned after all, and the pact, a Spaniard explains, was simply an agreement that if Ninica were not happy living in the country, she could return to the city. Now that she has returned, however, she plans to stay: "The one who left has al-ready left. . . . [But] your little animal returned. . . . The one who left wasn't yours, a person of the city, and the one who returned to remain with you forever is a little animal of the country."[31] The catastrophe of the derail-ment transformed Ninica and altered her marriage to Mauro from a tenuous agreement to a sacred promise.

Asturias refuses to simply end this play on the happy note of marriage renewed. Porfirión returns with the mask in his hands. His arm is bleed-ing, and the mask is covered with blood. Someone shot him, he says, when he came into the house to get the mask. He was shot as he ran from the house, and the mask needs to be cleaned to ensure that his wounds will not worsen. Porfirión, however, refuses to be treated and, like a wild animal, runs before Mauro can look at the wound.

This "first day of the world," as Ninica proclaims at the play's end, finds Mauro changed by the people around him and by his visits to the Chama Soluna. This mix of gypsies and peasants, Catholics and Mayans, criollos and indigenous, puts Mauro at the center of a world that seems caught between waking and dreaming and between rational and mystical existence. Mauro wants to believe the ideas of the people around him, but he sees Chama Soluna as only a person who has knowledge of the natural world. He is dismayed when he awakens to discover the prophesy of Ninica's return has not come true, but he does not take the dream with the seriousness as a sign in and of itself. He seems to desire the life force that the indigenous carry within them, but through his carelessness, he injures that of Porfirión.

Asturias also seems to be on the outside looking in, much in the same way that his autobiographical character does. According to Camayd-Freixas, Asturias had little contact with the indigenous people in Guatemala before he left to live in Europe.[32] Some have even suggested that his 1923 thesis on indigenous Guatemalans was superficial, even racist.[33] Asturias's view of the indigenous is filtered through European anthropology, through the lens of Reynaud.

Soluna itself seems to be more the product of a European worldview than a Mayan one. The happy ending, the trope of marriage or marriage reconciled, has long ended the comedies of Europe. Indeed, many of the elements of the play come from the European model of the well-made play, unlike *Hombres de maíz,* which critics praised because it seemed more organic, disjointed, and dreamlike. The play includes comic servants who explain the action of the play, colorful villagers who provide comic relief, and plot twists that, after a violent climax, end in happy resolution. The play follows the basic unities and only abandons verisimilitude during Mauro's "dream." Even the prophesy has a rational explanation in the end, the derailment providing cover for an otherwise implausible event.

In fact, as Gerald Martin suggests in the introduction of his translation of *Hombres de maíz,* much of what Asturias writes seems to spring from his personal life. Martin notes that the book was written during a difficult time for Asturias.[34] Here the parallel between Mauro and Asturias goes further. Asturias married, divorced, and turned to alcohol in the period between his return to Guatemala and the publication of the book. The image of the *tecuna* fleeing her husband echoes through his 1947 divorce, the book, as virtually all of the male characters pursue lost women, and the play *Soluna,* in which Mauro attempts to reconcile the forces that have taken Ninica from him. But by the time he wrote *Soluna,* Asturias had married his second wife, and the separation of Mauro and Ninica ends happily.

Soluna's ending also seems to belie Asturias's feeling of being a stranger in his own homeland. Mauro longs for the life force of people like Porfirión, but his lack of faith allows him to shoot the animal spirit. Porfirión appears like a ghostly reminder at the end, bleeding, wounded, but not getting close to Mauro, fleeing in the end rather than receiving treatment. Mauro stands in for Asturias as the walking dead. Everywhere, Asturias swims in the mythology of the indigenous people of his homeland, but the mythology will not flow through him in the way that he perceives it flows through the indigenous people.

Asturias's participation in the Guatemalan government has also recently been questioned. In a recent article in the *Jornada Semanal* (*The Weekly Journal*), Saúl Hurtado Heras depicts a man detached from his country's politics: Asturias did not sign the Manifesto of the 311, a document calling for the overthrow of the Ubico regime, and was content to serve as ambassador to France in 1966 during the height of bloody repression by a military government. This was despite the fact that Asturias had also worked as a cultural attaché for the democratic governments of the 1940s and 1950s, and he believed he was an advocate for the rights of the indigenous, which to Hurtado, seemed fickle.[35]

Indeed a recent resurgence in the popularity of Asturias has caused an intense debate. As more indigenous writers begin to find their own voice, they cite the lack of authenticity of the voice of a stand-in, a man who may look Mayan but who possesses an ultimately European gaze. As Mario Roberto Morales notes:

> There are other indigenous writers of today who demand authenticity in opposition to Asturias and who do not want to be called Indian but "Mayan," appealing to the idea of identity as a construct and to *political correctness,* and they accuse Asturias of being an ideologist of *ladino* racism, not only for his master's thesis, but for his misrepresentations of the native and the Mayan.[36]

Morales answers the detractors of Asturias and goes as far as to say that Asturias never sought to be a voice for the indigenous. Morales suggests that Asturias had a different project:

> Asturias continues being an inescapable point of reference and his literary defense constitutes not a defense of the ladinidad, its ethnocentrism, and its

presumed racism, but of the possibility necessary to construct a nationality, a nation, and a racially mixed, intercultural identity, in which the right to the exercising of cultural differences does not constitute a separatist practice, like in North American multiculturalism, but a way to integrate the components of transculturation. . . . Asturias incorporated the Mayan and indigenous into his identity and put it in the center of the Guatemalan identity . . .[37]

Asturias's Mayan characters, perhaps, stand as a simulacrum of the authentic Mayans, a shadow in danger of standing in for the real on the stage of world literature. But Asturias, in his quest for a national identity, for good or bad, appropriated the Mayan; his texts became a map of the criollo Guatemalan attempt to penetrate the indigenous culture and to construct a relationship of the people to the land.

Nationalist drama, like *Soluna,* employs a series of national metaphors that work together, and sometimes even in contradiction, to create an image of the nation at a particular moment. The drama must present an image acceptable to the citizens/audience. The dramatist traces the agreed-on boundaries of the nation by creating a space that contains the citizens, or rather a construction of what the dramatist believes the citizen to be.

A few dramas present a variety of characters in an attempt to construct a progressive concept of who belongs within the nation, such as Galich's multiracial fellowship. Although a few of the dramas do not specify the race of each character, several of them have specifically mestizo characters. Dramatic *mestizaje* creates a metaphor for a cohesive national people built out of specific racial stereotypes of both European and indigenous people. It creates an opening through which all people of the nation can feel a natural connection to the land of the nation, and it creates an identification for those of the current anti-imperialist struggle with indigenous peoples oppressed by the original colonization.

Metaphors of who belongs in the nation and where the nation exists do not work if their construction does not form part of a national sense of continuity. Creating an image of the nation inconsistent with prevailing ideas falls flat on the national audience. Dramatists may advance some new ideas in their plays, but most of the ideas explored are emergent. However, even with the historical break these works occupy, the images they create must appear to be in keeping with something eternal. The characters must enact events and reflect values that show the current national configuration to be the logical outcome of past events. The next section will explore the importance of creating a national history.

PART THREE
NICARAGUA: MAPPING OUT HISTORY

6 NICARAGUAN NATIONAL THEATRE

Theatre in Nicaragua developed in a way similar to the theatre in Guatemala, in that there was very little scripted performance of national works until the twentieth century. The linguistics scholar Daniel G. Brinton recorded a performance in Masaya, Nicaragua, of *El Güegüence,* the oldest surviving Nicaraguan drama, and translated it into English in 1883. The main character, Güegüence, comes before the colonial court to pay his taxes, and through his trickery, he manages to have his eldest son married to the governor's daughter. The dance drama is especially significant in that it is still performed on a regular basis today.

The play mixes Spanish language with the indigenous Nahuatl to create a play of words that is ultimately subversive. The poet and dramatist Pablo Antonio Cuadra said of this fusion that appears in several of the colonial *loas:*

> The Nicaraguans were a people passing slowly from one language to another. It was a meeting and the slow fusion of two languages and for various centuries it had been a mixture, a jargon as a result of this linguistic fusion. . . . Little by little Castilian dominated, but acquiring a great richness of words, turns of phrase, and syntactic liberties that explain the later expressive power of a Rubén Darío.[1]

Later nationalist movements attempted to recapture what they considered a specifically national language.

During the nineteenth century, Iberian theatre groups and circus performers toured Latin America. By the end of the century, several theatre houses had opened in Nicaragua, but they performed Peninsular plays or French plays translated into Spanish. A few Nicaraguans wrote plays as part of the debate between the Conservative and Liberal parties, each censoring the other's drama when in power.

In Guatemala, partisan conflict grew out of caudillo politics. Nicaraguans maintained a similar power balance between Liberals and Conservatives after the 1821 war of independence, but that power was the subject of much more direct intervention from the United States. In 1855 the conflict between the parties prompted the Liberal Party to invite the U.S. mercenary William Walker to depose the Conservative government. With the gold rush on, the United States began to look at Nicaragua as a possible canal site. A short seventeen miles of land stood between the Pacific Ocean and Lake Nicaragua, which drained into the Atlantic by the San Juan River. Walker received full support from the United States. He appointed himself president in 1856, made English the official language of Nicaragua, and reinstituted slavery. The combined efforts of armies from Nicaragua and Honduras drove Walker from Nicaragua. After Walker's continued attempts to retake Nicaragua and Honduras, he landed in British hands in 1860. The British handed him over to the Hondurans, who promptly executed him.

The United States sent troops to Nicaragua to intervene in the partisan warfare in 1857, and again in 1893. The United States also sent troops in 1909 to force then-president José Santos Zelaya to resign. A member of the Liberal Party, Zelaya aggressively engaged Nicaragua in developing export production. His program was "to devote as much of the government's resources as possible to the extension of the railway system, a network of highways, and port improvements, as well as to modernize the apparatus of the state and extend education and literacy."[2] He sought to develop Nicaragua from a monoculture of coffee and sugar production for the United States to a dynamic economic power. This program angered Conservatives, who preferred the current economic relationship with the United States. Zelaya secured loans from European governments and made overtures to countries other than the United States to build the canal. This, along with his meddling in the government of Honduras, prompted the United States to support a revolt in 1909, headed by the Conservative general Emiliano Chamorro. Chamorro named José María Estrada president, but the balance of power between the parties was fragile, and the Conservative government did not have the base of support that the Liberal party had secured. It would take the continued presence of the U.S. Marines in order to secure power for the Conservative faction. The U.S. Marines came again in 1912 to put down a Liberal rebellion and remained in Nicaragua until 1925. They again returned in 1926, remaining until 1933.

During the Conservative regime, marked most notably by the presidency of Adolfo Díaz, the United States aggressively pursued investment in the Nicaraguan economy. Loans were issued to aid Nicaragua in paying off other foreign debt and to keep the government solvent. The national bank and railway were offered as collateral. The United States obtained the rights to collection of duties, and the Díaz government signed the Bryan-Chamorro Treaty of 1914, giving the United States exclusive rights to build a canal. Within a few years, the Conservative government handed over a large portion of Nicaragua to U.S. control. According to Knut Walter in *The Regime of Anastasio Somoza, 1936–1956,* the Conservatives and the United States had a mutually beneficial relationship:

> From 1911 to 1927, the Nicaraguan faction that was willing to do whatever the United States required was the Conservative Party because it knew that support from Washington was vital to maintain its hold on government. But there was no fundamental quarrel between the Conservatives and the U.S. interest in Nicaragua, either. That U.S. corporations took over control of the national railroad and the national bank and that U.S. officials collected customs duties and determined government expenditures was of no great concern to the Conservative oligarchy from Granada. Not even national sovereignty meant much to the Conservatives who signed the Bryan-Chamorro Treaty in exchange for three million dollars. The fact of the matter was that Conservative government policy, in line with U.S. interests, was geared fundamentally to ensuring fiscal solvency and public order.[3]

The partisan warfare had left Nicaragua wide open to invasion. As the Guatemalan people also discovered, once the process of foreign investment had started, it was difficult for any Central American nation to govern itself. One party could always call on the United States for aid, and the United States would oblige to protect its interests. This history of U.S. intervention forms much of material mined by writers for the nationalist drama.

The *costumbres* of the early twentieth century fell into the categories of either political satires or poetic drama. The poetic drama drew inspiration from Nicaragua's national poet, Rubén Darío (1867–1916). Darío wrote a few plays himself, *Cada oveja . . . (Each Sheep . . .)* (performed in 1886), and *Manuel Acuña* (written in 1889 or 1890), about the tragic Mexican poet, but both plays are lost. Scholars speculate that he had begun a play called *La princesa está triste . . . (The Princess Is Sad . . .),* based on his poem *Sonatina,* but no evidence of that text has ever been found.[4]

Political satires reflected the continuing struggle between the warring factions, but they were mixed with themes of the opportunism of the emerging middle class. As political corruption became commonplace, more *costumbres* were written that featured aspiring young Nicaraguans who use the political situation to get ahead. Most notable of these was *La rifa* (*The Raffle*) (1909), by Anselmo Fletes Bolaños, writing under the pseudonym Gil Blas. The play involved young men attempting to marry into a wealthy family, the Palmiras, by lying about their professions. One young man, Juanelo, succeeds in winning the right to marry one of the Palmira girls, but he backs out when a more profitable political venture comes along.

As the United States gained more control of the Nicaraguan economy and political machinery, the Liberal party members were increasingly frustrated at their lack of access to the mechanisms of government. The Liberal faction, with its traders, laborers, and small coffee planters, needed a much more dynamic economy than the Conservative–U.S. alliance would allow.[5] In 1924, in elections supervised by the U.S. Marines, a bipartisan ticket of a Conservative president and Liberal vice president won the elections, defeating the popular Conservative candidate Emiliano Chamorro.

The Marines left Nicaragua in 1925, satisfied that the election had been fair and that stability had been restored. However, Chamorro, dissatisfied with the election results, took the government in a military coup. Word came from Washington that the United States would not support such action or recognize Chamorro's government. Chamorro agreed to step down, but instead of handing the government back to José Solórzano, the exiled president, or Juan Batista Sacasa, the vice president, Chamorro handed the government over to the Conservative Díaz, whom the United States did recognize. The outraged Liberal faction began a revolt, led by Sacasa and General José María Moncada, at the beginning of 1926.

As the Liberal rebellion gained momentum, Díaz invited the United States to intervene. Some scholars, such as Gregorio Selser, have asserted that the rebellion gained enough support to win the war with Díaz and the Marines. Moncada, however, interested only in striking a deal to gain the presidency for himself, slowed the efforts of the rebel forces. General Augusto Sandino, who joined the effort with his small army of men from the northern departments, wrote that he thought Moncada was trying to have him killed.[6] It was clear that Moncada knew who the most powerful player was on the field: the Coolidge-appointed mediator, Colonel Henry Stimson. Sandino, in his writings, and Gregorio Selser both assert that Moncada committed premeditated treason against the sovereignty of Nicaragua when the Liberal army negotiated a treaty with the Conservative government. In 1928 Moncada was elected president.

Augusto Sandino never stopped fighting against the Marines and the Conservative government officials who invited them. He fought and wrote over the next seven years, stating that his sole directive was to drive the Yankees from Nicaraguan soil. To Sandino, the enemy was clearly the United States and the traitors who fought with them: "On the same date at Santa Barbara, Jinotega jurisdiction, Colonel Juan Altamirano defeated the enemy who left on the battlefield five traitorous dogs and one Yankee pirate."[7] As the tactics of the U.S. Marines became more brutal in their war against Sandino, more people were compelled to join Sandino's cause.

Sandino attempted to appeal to the regionalism of fellow Latin Americans in his struggle. Certain that other republics would share the disdain for U.S. soldiers on Latin American soil, Sandino traveled all over Central America and wrote to the leaders of many of the Latin American states to secure military aid. None of his requests for aid were heeded, although a certain amount of unofficial aid, in the form of cash and weapons, came to the Sandinistas, and individuals from other countries joined his army. But heads of state were wary of endangering their own relationships with the United States. Thus, the regionalist spirit that enabled the Central American states to band together to defeat William Walker in the 1850s had been dampened by interference from the United States.

By 1930 the U.S. Marines had trained Nicaraguans to fight the war against Sandino. The Nicaraguan National Guard began to engage Sandino in the same brutal manner that the Marines had. With the National Guard replacing the Marines and arrangements for a second U.S.-supervised election under way, the Marines prepared to leave Nicaragua. Now, in addition to the economic imperialism from the United States and the unresolved partisan warfare, which had only been put on hold by U.S. control of the government, the United States left a military class that existed outside of the Nicaraguan constitution and beyond the control of the government.

Juan Batista Sacasa was elected in 1932. With the National Guard in place and a new president elected, the United States made good on its promise to withdraw from Nicaraguan soil. Augusto Sandino responded immediately, requesting peace talks that proved disastrous for him and his faction in the end. Knut Walter suggests that the historical and political fact of his request places Sandino within the context of caudillo warfare. His power lay primarily in the northernmost departments, and his written requests for conditions for peace stipulate the formation of a new state as a cooperative for his followers.[8] Regardless of the reality of Sandino's life and motives, his struggle against U.S. intervention and his writing on the sovereignty of Nicaragua have made him a national and regional hero.

Anastasio Somoza García, the newly appointed head of the National Guard, began taking advantage of his growing political power. He assassinated Sandino, initiated many attacks on Sandino's newly disarmed Army for the Defense of the National Sovereignty, and began using the National Guard for aggressive political campaigning. Somoza did not need to take the government by force. Enough Liberals and Conservatives alike felt that the chaos of partisan warfare and the war with Sandino needed to be remedied by a strong president. The playwright and poet Pablo Antonio Cuadra supported Somoza's presidency, believing that perhaps a fascist government or even a monarchy might be the only answer to the country's problems. Somoza also courted the United States, assuring the government that U.S. interests would be protected and that he would do their bidding. Somoza was even dubbed "the last Marine" by Nicaraguans, which provoked the famous statement from Roosevelt: "He may be a son-of-a-bitch, but he's *our* son-of-a-bitch."

Chronicling the involvement of the United States in Nicaraguan politics was Hernán Robleto (1895–1968). Originally Robleto wrote many *costumbres* after 1918 and staged them in his own venue, the Compañía Dramático Nacional. As Robleto matured as a playwright, his work became more political in nature. In 1930 he wrote the novel *Sangre en el trópico* (*Blood in the Tropics*), about the history of the U.S. interventions in Nicaragua. In 1936 he wrote the comic opera *Pájaros del norte* (*Birds of the North*), about the effects of the U.S. presence on Nicaraguan family and society. Robleto eventually went into exile after Somoza was elected.

On the Conservative side, a group of Nicaraguan writers began a movement to recover Nicaraguan culture in 1935. Pablo Antonio Cuadra, Joaquín Pasos (1915–1947) and José Coronel Urtecho (1906–) formed the Nicaraguan vanguard movement, or the Vanguardia, in response to a perceived lack of Nicaraguan culture and a general tendency to imitate the culture of the Peninsula. All members of the Conservative party, the men of the Vanguardia felt that the Liberal party and the foreign capitalists were destroying the fiber of Nicaraguan society by breaking down the relationship between *patrón* and peasant. The Vanguardia's recovery of

Nicaraguan culture was an attempt to revive the values of the social structure. This nationalist cultural movement was very conservative, as opposed to the radical movement in Guatemala during the country's nationalist period.

Although the Vanguardia attempted to create a national theatre in Nicaragua, they were unsuccessful. Their original manifesto called for a theatre to be opened in every town to facilitate new works along with the older popular and colonial performances. The Vanguardia originally supported Somoza, believing that only a strong government could manage the centrifugal tendencies of Nicaraguan politics. Somoza, however, had no interest in theatre or in a national culture.

During the Somoza regime, the National Guard suppressed any plays that were openly critical of the government. Plays that were written by Nicaraguans could only make veiled references to the political situation and could only comment on corruption in Latin America in a very general sense. For instance, in 1943 Enrique Fernández Morales (1918–1982) wrote *La niña del río (Child of the River)*. The play flashes back to the life of Rafaela Herrera, called upon to defend the mouth of the San Juan River against the invading British in 1762 after her father died moments before the attack. The play clearly takes an anti-imperialist stance against foreign invasion, perhaps in reaction to Somoza's policy of close alliance with the United States and with U.S. capitalists.

Somoza, and the Somoza dictators who came after him, used considerable force to stay in power. There is a broad constellation of forces that created some of the brutal dictatorships in Latin America; to many it is puzzling that the crafters of U.S. foreign policy who spoke so passionately about exporting democracy supported some of these regimes. The combined fear of communism and the desire for economic dominance made stability the primary consideration of the U.S. administration. This emphasis on stability resulted in U.S. support for some of the most oppressive dictators in Latin American history. The United States supported Somoza and both of his sons: Luis and Anastasio Jr.

In the 1950s and 1960s, several theatre companies were formed in the metropolitan areas of Nicaragua. The level of theatrical activity rose in the country, although theatre companies produced mostly foreign plays.[9] A national theatre was built in Managua in 1971, during the regime of Anastasio Somoza Debayle, the younger of the two sons. The economic situation of the poor, however, caused a public outcry against the expense of the structure, which cost two and a half million U.S. dollars.[10]

Rolando Steiner (1936–1987) and Alberto Ycaza (1945–2002), playwrights who also founded theatre companies in the 1960s, drew their inspiration primarily from European forms. Solórzano places Steiner within the postwar period because his work dealt with universal themes. Steiner's play *Judit* (1957) features a man who, bored with his marriage, creates an imaginary woman. His attempts to destroy his dream life, however, cause the destruction of his reality.[11] A year after the election of Luis Somoza, the elder of Anastasio Somoza's two sons, Steiner wrote *Antígona en el infierno* (*Antigone in Hell*) (1958) as a commentary on the continuing repression of the Somoza dynasty. Although the play deals with the same general issues as Sophocles' play, it focuses on the repression and torture exercised by the dictator Creon, a representation of the Somozas.

Anti-Communist policy makers in the United States asserted that the Cuban Revolution would have a "domino effect," and they blamed the influence of the Cuban Communists for the Sandinista Revolution in Nicaragua in 1979. The momentum for the Sandinista Revolution (named for Sandino) built in the 1970s when Anastasio Somoza Debayle had alienated much of the support for the government by using his office and his connections with foreign capitalists to further his own gains. Much of the business sector, which had supported the Somoza dynasty in the past, allied with the growing resistance. The corruption that followed a 1972 earthquake fanned the flames of this trend.

When the earthquake leveled much of Managua and the outlying areas, relief poured into the country from around the world. Somoza Debayle owned many of the businesses involved in reconstructing the damage, and this inevitably provided him with an excuse to divert the funds to his personal accounts. With Somoza Debayle's base of support shrinking, his repressive measures against the opposition became more frequently exercised. The old part of Managua is still empty and still open because hardly anything was rebuilt in the area after the earthquake. The only building "downtown" that survived the earthquake was, ironically, the Bank of America.

After the 1979 revolution, the Sandinista government did two things that facilitated a sudden growth in theatre: it launched a massive, and very successful, literacy campaign, and it established a Ministry of Culture as part of the cabinet. Initially, before the war with the United States began in 1982, the Sandinistas provided ample funding for cultural activities through the Asociación Sandinista Trabajadores Culturales (ASTC). Much of the local cultural activity, which had been germinating during the revolutionary struggle, began to sprout into a popular cultural revival.

Although scholars often cite Alan Bolt (1951?–) as a leader in modern Nicaraguan theatre, much of this local theatre is collective in nature, and there are many other groups that use performance as a pedagogical tool. Bolt's group, Nixtayolero, operated out of a small community outside of Matagalpa, in the northern mountains, and began by using theatre as a tool for agrarian education. Many of the group's projects were political as well and drew criticism from the Sandinista government that supported it.[12]

The United States initially remained tolerant of the Sandinista government and its mild reforms. However, the agrarian reforms, designed to aid the small coffee and cotton producers, angered U.S. capitalists. By the 1980s the CIA had grown considerably more skilled in its covert operations. Although the United States supported the contra army against the Nicaraguan government, operations remained at a low level of terrorism in the north, combined with an economic embargo to destabilize the economy. The United States succeeded in intimidating the Nicaraguan people into voting for a U.S.-funded coalition of the political opposition parties. It is not surprising that the U.S. Marines timed the invasion of Panama to occur just two months before the Nicaraguan elections of 1990. Nicaraguan national drama provides a sense of Nicaraguan national history. The plays draw a timeline for the audience and give the nation a sense of continuity.

National History

National culture carves out spatial boundaries of the nation in the present, but in doing so it must draw the temporal boundaries of the nation as well. This explains, to some degree, why so many nationalist plays deal specifically with historical events. Although the citizens in the audience may view themselves as coming together to celebrate the history of the nation and the revolution that liberated it, the drama represents a negotiation between high cultural forces seeking prevalence for their own particular view of national history. The view of the nation's history that resonates with the audience the most will, for the time being, become canon. When we examine nationalist plays that are set in the past, we must consider the relationship of history to the present in terms of *which* present and also, more aptly, *whose* present. For the builders of the nation, dramatic accounts of its history pull together what ends are left loose by dramatic national metaphors.

In his 1882 essay "What Is a Nation?" Ernst Renan suggests, as many nationalist writers believe, that the nation is defined by its history when he asserts that there are two phenomena that create a nation:

> One is the possession in common of a rich legacy of memories; the other is present-day consent, the desire to live together. . . . The nation, like the individual, is the culmination of a long past of endeavors, sacrifice and devotion. . . . To have common glories in the past and to have a common will in the present; to have performed great deeds together, to wish to perform still more—these are essential conditions for being a people.[13]

The dramatist would naturally seek to memorialize events important to the formation of the nation.

Specifically, with the historical break expressed through revolution, the national historical drama has the effect of establishing a needed feeling of continuity. Spencer E. Roberts, in *Soviet Historical Drama*, states that after the Russian Revolution, Soviet leaders became interested in Russian history. Roberts understands the apparent contradiction between a revolutionary movement and the use of the past, given that a revolution "breaks the continuity, rejects the past in the name of the future, and is hostile to historical traditions."[14] Roberts feels that the revolutionary government used Russian history to bolster its own legitimacy:

> Concomitantly with their efforts to inspire in the Soviet mind an awareness of continuity between the progressive forces of the past and those of the present the Marxist leaders enlisted the services of history for another reason. By inculcating a sense of continuity, the government could expect to persuade some wavering, or even hostile, segments of the population to accept the new order; but something greater was needed to inspire those previously uncommitted groups to cherish and defend the new state. This might be achieved by stressing the common past of the members of the new society.[15]

The citizens of the new Soviet state needed to feel solidarity with one another, that they had been through a common past. Furthermore, they needed to believe that the revolution was the logical outcome of the nation's past.[16] The celebratory nature of nationalist drama in dealing with historical themes, and the importance given to certain events or people in constructing this common past, becomes part of the process of creating a national mythology from the national history.

These ideas are echoed by Jeffrey D. Mason in his book about drama in the United States, *Melodrama and the Myth of America.* Although Mason examines a different genre performed in a developed country, he illuminates national theatre's potential to bind a community and to create a sense of continuity and progress. Mason articulates what previous scholars struggled with in terms of the public nature of the performed event and what it means for community identification:

> If ... I study the performances of American plays, written on American subjects and produced in America by American artists and for American audiences, and enjoying long and successful runs because of the enthusiastic support of those audiences, I am studying what certain Americans wanted other Americans, and the world at large, to believe and that they believed about America as such. Theatre becomes an intricate and reflexive exercise in cultural self-definition. . . . If we draw too clear a distinction between the artists as producers . . . and the audience as consumers . . . we are locating the process in a somewhat artificially limited temporal and causal framework, for those artists created what they believe, based on past experience, will elicit a certain kind of response from the audience. The interaction is continuous and infinite.[17]

This continuous loop brings into play cultural metaphors that are already operative within the minds of the citizen/audience member. A playwright must write on the basis of what the audience knows to be true or the play will not run long, if it is ever produced. Thus, the historical myths must evolve out of the collective myths of the theatregoers. As Mason says, "To contact many minds at once, myth must employ a semiotic repertoire that time and usage have hallowed and rendered widely accessible, so a mythology is a composition of cultural metaphors."[18] The history of the nation must be an agreed-upon history.

The use of a national history in drama, then, can help people make sense of the present. Particularly if there has been a historical break, such as a revolution, the reconfiguring of the national history can create a sense of continuity and therefore legitimacy. Representing the past can bind a people, giving them a common origin, uniting them within the borders of the nation. In Nicaragua and Guatemala, this process takes on particular urgency in the wake of foreign imperialism.

Seamus Deane, when writing about Irish nationalism, describes the quest of the Irish for a national culture. The quest becomes all the more imperative when the national culture has been wiped out by a colonizing force: "At its most powerful, colonialism is a process of radical dispossession. A colonized people are without a specific history and even, as in Ireland and other cases, without a specific language."[19] With colonial interruption and appropriation, the project becomes one of creating a sense of the nation as self-evident. This has its consequences: "insurgent nationalisms attempt to create a version of history for themselves in which their intrinsic essence has always manifested itself, thereby producing readings of the past that are as monolithic as that which they are trying to supplant."[20] Nationalist historical drama in postcolonial nations has a particular rhetorical function: to serve the purposes of nation building and to rewrite the history that (nationalists believe) colonial or imperialist forces wrote.

(Re)presenting the History of the Nation

To better understand the ways nationalist drama serves these purposes, it is beneficial to understand some possible motivations for turning to the past. David Lowenthal creates a model in *The Past Is a Foreign Country* to explain how we cognitively organize the past and why we seek to preserve it. His categories of the benefits of the past are familiarity, reaffirmation and validation, identity, guidance, enrichment, and escape. Not all the categories are useful when thinking about nationalist theatre. Enrichment and escape assume a positive or negative moral motivation for seeking the past, as does the concept of moral guidance, and they have little bearing on the workings of the formation of a national identity. Therefore, I will examine the possibilities of the first three categories.

Lowenthal believes that the past provides a sense of familiarity. We use the past to render the present familiar. In a revolutionary culture, a historical drama aids the citizen/audience member in feeling at home within the new culture. Historical drama can be used to explain the revolution in a way that makes sense in the context of a prerevolutionary society.

Lowenthal believes that using the past can provide a sense of reaffirmation and validation: "The past validates present attitudes and actions by affirming their resemblance to former ones."[21] The scenes of the past in historical drama validate current attitudes held by the revolutionary culture. Ideas that necessitate the revolutionary break are projected back to exist before the revolution or before imperialism.

By identification, Lowenthal means both individual and community identity. The metaphors outlined in chapter 4 and 5 of this book demonstrate how a people define themselves at that historical moment.

However, part of that momentary self-definition entails the history from which the collective has emerged. Lowenthal states:

> Awareness of history likewise enhances communal and national identity, legitimating a people in their own eyes. . . . Groups lacking a sense of their own past are like individuals who know nothing of their parents.[22]

Lowenthal feels that people of postcolonial nations express this need to know the national history most strongly because:

> Identification with a national past often serves as an assurance of worth against subjugation or bolsters a new sovereignty. Peoples deprived by conquest of their proper past strive hard to retrieve its validating comforts.[23]

The project of establishing a national history takes on a particular urgency in the postcolonial context.

Lowenthal believes that sequence is one of the attributes that we appreciate about the past, that is, the fact that we give everything an ordered chronology and organize the past into durations of time. National historical drama configures history into a history of the revolution with events leading up to the revolutionary moment. By ordering the nation's history on the stage, the dramatist can use the past to help the citizen/audience member feel a sense of familiarity in a changing culture. The national drama validates the new values by demonstrating their existence in the past and by giving the citizens a picture of the past with which they can identify. The national drama lends continuity to a fractured and changing landscape of the national history.

7   ALAN BOLT AND IDENTIFICATION WITH THE STRUGGLE IN *BANANA REPUBLIC*

After the Sandinista Revolution of 1979, the new Nicaraguan government made financial support available to any group that wished to form a theatre troupe. Professionals and amateurs alike made use of this program, and troupes sprang up around the country to aid a variety of causes, from literacy to agrarian reform to ending domestic violence. It was under these auspices that Alan Bolt took over the Nixtayolero theatre company, which in the Nahuatl language means "New Dawn."[1] Bolt had plenty of experience with political theatre work before he took over the company in 1981.

Bolt cofounded the Teatro Estudiantil Universitario (TEU) in 1971 in reaction to actions of the Somoza regime against the university:

> On the occasion of a celebrated student strike in 1971, because of the expulsion of two university leaders, it became necessary to organize the population of students by any means, and with them, to exert pressure on the University Meeting so that the decree was revoked. And, in those days, the TEU (Teatro Estudiantil Universitario) was born as an agitation and propaganda group. The strike did not prevail but the agitacional capacity of the theater had been demonstrated and the group began to form.[2]

Bolt directed several pieces for the group as it toured to various national theatre festivals. He lists a few in his article on the TEU in *Conjunto: El obispo* (*The Bishop*), *Paraíso perdido siglo XX* (*Paradise Lost Twentieth Century*), and *Poemas indígenas* (*Indigenous Poems*). The group also performed some pieces that are based in the scripture, both Christian and Mayan: *Génesis* (which caused a scandal with a nude scene) and *El evangelio según San Lucas* (*The Gospel According to St. Luke*). The group also developed scenes around current issues: the rise in gasoline prices, the hospital workers' strike, the expulsion of students, and the proliferation of drugs.[3]

The Somoza regime jailed the student theatre group, and it was not until students and faculty alike exerted pressure on the government that the thespians were released. Bolt continued to organize political theatre until he was forced underground in 1973.

Bolt then spent time in Masaya, organizing the Sandinista resistance. It was there, according to Adam Versényi, that Bolt began to understand the importance of indigenous culture and of using it in his own theatre practice.[4] Bolt began to see indigenous culture as an essential component in Nicaraguan identity. Bolt was committed to incorporating both indigenous and European tradition as a means to finding the Nicaraguan future. As Bolt stresses:

> I believe sincerely that we must study our origins and what survives of our traditions: the festivals, passion plays, folkloric dances and songs, religious processions, the bull-deer dance, *El Güegüense* and all popular artistic forms, in order to incorporate them into our dramatic art, establishing a bridge of union between the past and the future, planting our work in those solidly rooted theatrical forms.[5]

After the triumph of the revolution in 1979, Bolt returned from Costa Rica, where he had lived in exile. He worked at the Ministry of Culture, running the theatre school until 1980, when he abandoned his high-profile post to take over Nixtayolero in the Matagalpa District. Bolt felt the need to return to grassroots theatre work.[6]

Nixtayolero was then run by Carida Chao Carbonero, a Cuban director from the Teatro Escambray. The group was on a small coffee farm near the town of Matagalpa, and the theatre work centered on issues of coffee production.[7] Bolt began to expand the group's charter to include issues of domestic violence, sustainable agriculture, and government corruption. According to Versényi, the members of Nixtayolero would sometimes live in a community in order to better understand the issues the people there faced.[8]

Bolt would develop a piece collaboratively and then do the final writing himself.[9] Initially, Bolt's work supported the basic platform of the Sandinista Party. *Morir es difícil* (*Dying Is Difficult*), written in the 1970s, tells the story of a poor peasant woman who is dying. Her family is too poor to pay the funeral expenses. The woman laments that she will not live long enough to see the triumph of the revolution. Bolt ties the Sandinistas to their namesake when the woman's husband recounts to her his stories of fighting with Sandino in the 1920s.

One of Bolt's better-known plays, from the 1980s, *Ojo al Cristo* (*Watch Out for Christ*), also emphasized the importance of the revolution.[10] The members of Nixtayolero developed the piece in response to the corruption of the administration and the disempowerment of the workers at the collective Unidad de Producción Económica (Unit of Economic Production). According to Claudia Kaiser-Lenoir, the piece incorporated the past oppression under Somoza in a dream sequence to help the workers make sense of the present. The play stressed that no one could afford to remain apathetic or the gains of the revolution could be lost. In fact, one must stay vigilant in order to ever push for further reform.[11] Bolt's pieces continually make use of the past to make the present intelligible.

Alan Bolt's *Banana Republic* (1982) shows the sequence of events that led to the Sandinista Revolution. Through the portrayal of past events, Bolt enabled the audience to identify with the past and to view it as the logical precursor to the Sandinista victory. Bolt's company toured this play, and its confirmation by the masses made it a reclamation of a national past that the Sandinistas felt had been miswritten by foreign imperialists. The play established the Nicaraguan identity framed within the Sandinista ideological platform.

The play begins with the performers entering dressed like vaudeville or circus performers. The master of ceremonies, or Prólogo, acts as a barker, announcing the various acts that the company has to offer. Most of them are humorous renditions of circus acts: the brothers with the "rhythm of Puerto Rico in their hips"; "Magnet Man" from the "mysterious world of Africa," to which the barker adds that people should keep an eye on their wallets; a strong man who is a mix of "Batman, Superman, Aquaman[,] and all the other men that there are," but who cannot lift the three-thousand-pound weight until Prólogo helps him; and Juan Chinga, a martial arts specialist who is the "heir to Bruce Lee."[12] Bolt felt that the humorous use of popular entertainment forms would get the attention of the people when the group performed their pieces on the street.

The players then performed a series of scenes to give the audience an overview of the nation's history. Prólogo informs the audience:

> the history that we come to tell you is a history of how some rich guys wanted to seize the land of the Indians, the history of how the blond foreigners invaded us, and of how our people rose up. . . . But you will see for yourself.[13]

The scenes draw upon popular mythology surrounding the evolution of the Sandinista struggle. The audience members identify with this popular view of the nation's past, both because of the popularity of the myths and because the figures of the popular legends are poor peasants or act on behalf of peasants and laborers.

For instance, in the first scene, the wealthy Spanish women lament that they do not have luxuries, such as Italian shoes and French hats. The wars of independence left them poor. Don Frutos, a *patrón,* explains that growing coffee will make them rich. "Coffee is now gold" that will enable them to build "palaces and cathedrals."[14] Unfortunately, the indigenous people have all the best land. Frutos explains that the land will be theirs after they write a law and impose taxes.

At the announcement of the new taxes, the indigenous characters worry that they will not be able to pay. Julian Roque, a leader of an indigenous uprising well known to the Nicaraguan audience, answers that they have hands, feet, blood, and justice, foreshadowing the events that a Nicaraguan audience would anticipate; Frutos defends the government's policy of putting the indigenous people to work, providing what is basically slave labor in building Nicaragua's infrastructure. In the next scene, two indigenous characters talk of the dangerous work in the mines. Generally, the indigenous characters speak with a dialect, but here one speaks in Nahuatl and the other translates into Spanish.

In the next scene, Prólogo talks about the rebellion that quickly spread from village to village. The government forces quash the rebellion when they capture and execute the leader, Roque. As he is about to be executed, Roque tells a joke normally attributed to Hatuey, the indigenous Cuban chief killed by colonial authorities in Cuba. The bishop tells Roque that he should be saved before being executed so that he can go to heaven. Roque asks if Christians go there when they die. When the bishop tells him they do, Roque declares that he would rather go to hell than be with assassins in heaven. The members of the audience would be familiar with this joke and would recognize its appropriateness in the scene, but they would also feel some identification with the indigenous people who struggled against colonial authority.

The audience would also be familiar with the following brief sketches of the gains made by Zelaya and the legendary defeat of Zeledón at Masaya. The scene with Zelaya heralds the rise of the Liberal party as Zelaya proclaims: "Progress, Work, Liberty." This draws a response from the Conservative Frutos: "Whisky, Order, Women, Money,"[15] lampooning the Conservatives' self-serving platform. Zelaya separates church and state, provides universal education, and legalizes divorce. However, his declaration that he will seek alliances with countries other than the United States brings about, in the next scene, the appearance of Imperialismo, the character who represents the new imperial power, the United States.

Imperialismo commands Zelaya to leave, whereupon Imperialismo replaces him with the loyal Díaz. Díaz repeats the refrain from the first scene, lusting after shoes from Italy and hats from France. As Prólogo explains, for Díaz to get what he wants, he allows Nicaragua to be turned into a "banana republic."[16]

The most significant part of the story is how the events of the Liberal uprising of 1926–27 bring about the historic struggle by Sandino's army. The play goes into some detail using a chorus, bringing to mind the chorus of Greek tragedy, to tell the story of how Sandino would not quit fighting even while Moncada made a deal. When Sandino agrees to put down his arms at the news that the U.S. Marines have left, the people try to stop him from going to Managua: "Don't go, General. Don't go. They are traitors. Don't go."[17] He mimes signing the pact with Sacasa, but as he exits, he is assassinated.

Bolt draws the struggle of Sandino through to the present struggle as he recounts the assassination of Somoza by the poet Rigoberto López, which does not bring about the end of the Somoza dynasty. As Luis and then Somoza Debayle become the next dictators, the character Imperialismo echoes the famous remark: "They may be sons-of-bitches, but they are *our* sons-of-bitches." Historically, this was spoken of their father by Franklin Roosevelt, but Bolt uses it here to show the continued support of the United States for the next Somoza dictator.

The play leads the audience up to the point of revolution, as the people and the chorus sing that they will fight for their country "if by sea in a warship, if by land in a military train" and they request that the audience not cry for them if they die.[18] With the revolution just a few years behind them, the play creates a continuity of history but also points to the continuation of the struggle with the Contra War just under way.

Bolt also makes a point of criticizing other playwrights when he lampoons artists who were loyal to the Somoza regime. A scene that portrays the intellectual movement of the 1930s clearly attacks the Vanguardia for its support of Somoza. The work of Cuadra and the other Vanguardia artists would also be recognizable to the audience, and Bolt's exaggeration of their position would be in keeping with the current Sandinista party line. Although Cuadra later changed his position with regard to the Somoza dictatorship, *Banana Republic* was performed at a time when Cuadra was at odds with the Sandinistas, a fact that is widely known because of Cuadra's use of the county's opposition newspaper to express his views.

The use of the popular form of street performance and the popular stories of national history give the Nicaraguan audience a sense of familiarity about the past and about the Sandinista regime, which purports to have grown from that past. The use of legend to perform the national history serves the specific function of identification. Popular myth gives the audience a way into the performance, a way to participate through its knowledge. The play forms a link in the chain of repetition of myth, reflecting back to the audience members what they already know to be true about the national history.

The audience will also identify with specific characters from the national history. The protagonists are always poor or fighting on behalf of the poor; they are people with whom the peasant, mestizo audience members would identify. Central to the play is the character of Sandino, the legendary figure from whom the Sandinistas take their name. The scenes with Sandino portray him as a poor, mestizo man fighting unselfishly for the sovereignty of the nation.

The members of the audience can identify with Sandino's struggle. Sandino fought the U.S. Marines in the 1930s, and the people who Bolt's performance troupe visited most likely participated in the 1970s struggle against the United States–backed Somoza Debayle. As Nicaragua entered the 1980s, the northern villages saw direct conflict with U.S.-trained and -funded contras. The play tells their own story of a continuous struggle of the people against foreign domination from colonization to its logical conclusion in the 1979 revolution. Foreign domination is personified in both blond gringos and the Conservative leaders whom they manipulate. The continuity of the identification with the Sandinista cause grants legitimacy to the then current Sandinista government.

With the purchase of a new farm outside of Matagalpa in 1984, Nixtayolero began to look for ways to become self-sufficient. This became a greater necessity when the funding situation became decentralized: the group's funding was moved in 1986 from the Ministry of Culture to the cultural workers' union and was moved again in 1988, when the government cut funding to cultural workers but created an Institute of Culture, which funneled money from international sources directly to the theatre groups. Randy Martin posits that this movement away from a direct relationship with the Sandinista Party led to a greater independence of criticizing the party's policies. Bolt has always had a somewhat contentious, albeit friendly, relationship with the Sandinistas and has even seemed to pride himself on being the gadfly that attempted to spur the party to change.[19]

Today, Nixtayolero has moved its base of operations to Managua and continues to win international acclaim. Bolt continues to do both theatre and environmental work, and he lives in Matagalpa.

Continuity Through Projection

Banana Republic provides a sense of identification with the past and with the present regime. Guatemala experienced a similar reconfiguration of national history through theatre. The Guatemalan play *El tren amarillo* (*The Yellow Train*) validates the values of the then current revolutionary culture through its examination of events preceding the Guatemalan Revolution of 1944. Written by Manuel Galich in the 1950s, *El tren amarillo* retraces the history of a Guatemala under imperialism, or more specifically, under the economic and political domination of the Boston-based United Fruit Company. The play also creates a sense of both national history and national continuity shared by the citizens/audience members.

El tren amarillo represents a Guatemala that existed before the economic domination by the United Fruit Company. The revolutionary government is legitimized through continuity. The national culture existed before United Fruit and persists under its exploitation. Galich does not portray the national culture as a recent creation. Rather, Galich's drama reproduces and reinforces the belief in the Guatemalan nation as a real entity that existed all along. The play reflects an idea of the Guatemalan nation as eternal. The play also presents the nation's liberation from foreign domination as the only logical choice for its people. The historical nature of *El tren amarillo* would provide a Guatemalan audience a reenactment of how Guatemala survived the abuse of U.S. imperialists, a testimony of the trials to which the people of the nation were subjected. Enough time had passed between the coup and the writing of the play that the events could be memorialized, agreed upon by the audience, and preserved in drama for later generations.

In this way, nationalist drama presents its audience with a stable and recognizable nation, even at a moment of national redefinition, such as a revolution. It provides clear boundaries between what belongs within nation and what belongs without. In the drama, the character of the nation remains unchanged by both foreign pressure and the movement of time, although this conception of the national character and national history may depart radically from subsequent conceptions by its artists and their audiences.

The drive for continuity appears in the text of Galich's narrative as he joins in the continuous action of refiguring the past. In act 1, Galich presents a clear vision of his ideal of the nation before the arrival of the company La Bananera: a map for Guatemalan spectators on which they can locate themselves in opposition to the outsiders of Bomb and Mariano. Acts 2 and 3 feature Galich's Guatemalans under pressure, forced to deal with situations that, in the context of the drama, seem inherently un-Guatemalan. Through the structure of the drama, Galich creates the sense that the nation and its people continue from the Guatemalan past into the present.

Galich validates the current regime when he projects the sense of racial solidarity back onto the 1920s and 1930s. In the play, the company managers from the United States import racism. When Whip refuses to allow the use of the company car to rescue the wounded Johnson because he is black, the other planters are stunned. It did not occur to them that Johnson's race would be an issue.

But in the time in which the play is set, Guatemala was still run by a few white landowners and class divisions ran along racial lines. Galich refigured history to be continuous with his revolutionary ideal. As Guatemala began to experience mass political participation in the 1940s and 1950s, and as people of different races became visible participants in the political process, more classes of people were included in the concept of the Guatemalan people. Galich wrote his modern 1950s vision of a multiracial fellowship back onto the 1920s and 1930s, a time when such a fellowship did not exist. Projecting such contemporary ideas back onto the past lends a certain amount of continuity to what are actually shifting definitions: it is like this now, and it was always like this. The historical drama, structured in this manner, provides the contemporary audience with events of the past with which they can more readily identify. The audience can feel that the integral and unchanging character of the nation has come through to the present.

While *El tren amarillo* projects racial solidarity back onto the past, Miguel Ángel Asturias's play *Audencia de los confines* uses the issues of the struggle of Guatemala's indigenous people. In *Audencia,* the corrupt colonial government develops a scheme to steal gold and women from the indigenous people, as the Dominican priest Bartolomé de las Casas works to free the indigenous people from slavery. Asturias portrays the priest as kind and fearless. In contrast, the colonial governor is deceitful and ruthless and his staff incompetent.

Written during a time of Guatemalan progressives' renewed interest in the plight of indigenous people, *Audencia* validates the contemporary attitude of racial solidarity and identification with the indigenous struggle. Asturias presents Las Casas as the play's hero, and he presents the governor, a representation of a government profiting from foreign domination, as its villain. The play also contains a warning. When Las Casas tells the indigenous character Nabori that he is free, the governor becomes angry: "Your laws! Your new laws! Papers! Papers!"[20] Indeed later the New Laws of Las Casas were so altered that they were ineffectual: slavery of the indigenous people continued in many forms. Asturias warns his contemporaries that vigilance is needed to ensure the liberty of the Mayans.

In Nicaragua, Rolando Steiner uses a similar anachronism in *La noche de Wiwilí* (1982) to affirm the gender-inclusive platform of the Sandinista Party. At the end of the play, the women raise the Sandinista flag and march to join the men who are fighting. In the 1930s, the time in which the play was set, women did not participate significantly in armed conflict. They did, however, play a decisive role in the Sandinista Revolution of 1979, three years before the play was published. Steiner highlights the role of women in 1979 by projecting it back onto the events of 1934.

Projecting such contemporary ideas back onto the past lends a certain amount of continuity to what are actually shifting definitions. When the historical drama is structured in this manner, the contemporary audience can more readily identify with the events of the past and can feel that the integral and unchanging character of the nation has come through to the present.

Following his analysis of the benefits of the past, Lowenthal outlines the valued attributes of the past. The names he chooses to ascribe to these attributes belie a tension between continuity and discontinuity: antiquity, continuity, termination, and sequence. On the one hand, the past leads to the present; on the other hand, the present is a break with the past.

Lowenthal asserts that we appreciate the remoteness of the past, but we also appreciate how the past provides a sense of precedence:

> Antiquity's chief use is to root credentials in the past. Nations and individuals habitually trace back their ancestry, institutions, culture, ideals to validate claims to power, prestige, and property. . . . Precedence evince the concern to demonstrate a heritage, a lineage, a claim that antedates others . . . .[21]

Certainly, nationalist drama would turn to the past to show how the current configuration of the nation and its people have existed before foreign imperialism. The characters in *Banana Republic* show a precedence, a lineage, of the Sandinista party and the free Nicaraguan nation, just as the characters in *El tren amarillo* represent the Guatemalan character that preceded the United Fruit Company.

The same holds true for Lowenthal's discussion of continuity and the "community of descent" that "connects the earliest folk with the latest folk."[22] Although Lowenthal asserts that appreciation of antiquity motivates the "restoration" of a structure to its original form, whereas continuity motivates the preservation of the changes the structure has undergone through time, both attributes offer the same legitimating power to the current regime. As Lowenthal points out:

> The accretive past is appreciated less for its own sake than because it has led to the present; Napoleon and Louis Philippe both emphasized the continuity of their national lineage to show French history culminating with themselves.[23]

If the history of Nicaragua culminates in the Sandinista Revolution of 1979, as in *Banana Republic,* or if the history of Guatemala's relationship with United Fruit ends with the revolution of 1944, as in *El tren amarillo,* then the revolution is part of the natural progression of events.

The past can now be interpreted and ordered in its relationship to the present. The past seems incapable of being changed, and history seems impervious to alteration. A nation's history, regardless of how nationalists reinterpret it, has the illusion of being incapable of reinterpretation. The attribute of sequence, the recognition that some events come before and lead to others, enables us, in the words of Lowenthal, "to shape memory, secure identity, and generate tradition."[24] Conversely, Lowenthal regards termination as a valued attribute of the past. A sense of completion gives the past order. We have emerged from something, broken with what has come before. The ambivalent representations of the revolution as a logical outcome of the nation's history and as a break with that history plays out in the works of various nationalist writers and constitutes part of the ambivalent character of the nation.

This tension belies a Marxist approach to the revolution as both the desired logical outcome of the progression of class struggle and the break from the hegemony of the national bourgeoisie. This historical, materialist approach always legitimates the current revolutionary regime and is often consciously used by writers who are influenced by Marxist ideas.[25]

However, writers who often do not support the current regime, or the current configuration of the nation, represent the revolutionary break in very different terms. Some nationalist writers may represent the revolution as part of the natural progression of class struggle, a natural throwing-off of an unnatural foreign economic domination, but a few have represented the revolution as a Freudian cycle of violent patricide that threatens to destroy the nation.[26]

(Re)presenting the Revolution

The Marxist approach, based in historical materialism, follows the notion that history is based on class struggle. As Marx states in the *Manifesto of the Communist Party*:

> The history of all hitherto existing society is the history of class struggles. Freeman and slave, patrician and plebeian, lord and serf, guild-master and journeyman, in a word, oppressor and oppressed stood in constant opposition to one another, carried on an uninterrupted, now hidden, now open fight, a fight that each time ended, either in a revolutionary reconstitution of society at large, or in the common ruin of the contending classes.[27]

Marx goes on to explain how the bourgeoisie developed and how the next class struggle must necessarily be between the bourgeoisie and the proletariat. He outlines how the bourgeoisie has brought about the conditions for its own downfall. Manuel Galich and Alan Bolt both wrote the revolution as part of the natural progression of economic relationships. The heroes of their nationalist drama are the proletarians who become politicized after suffering the oppression of foreign capitalists.

Galich, closely associated with President Jacobo Arbenz, was probably aware when he wrote *El tren amarillo* of the writings of Marx and the materialist understanding of historical events. As the plot of the play progresses, it follows the Marxist evolution of economic relationships. His characters in act 1, set in the 1920s and 1930s, are common peasants trying to make a living on the small parcels of land that they hold. By the 1940s, a generation later, struggling under the greedy policies of United Fruit, the Guatemalans begin to understand that nothing could save their class, and therefore nation, except a full-scale revolt.

Canche, a natural leader of his fellow workers, decides that the workers will stop working until the company improves the working conditions, a decision that earns him the label of "Communist" from his father, the superintendent. While his father decides to have Canche murdered, the action of the play is in the past, and the audience understands that the outcome of the events is the revolution of 1944. But, the revolt is not just a class war. For Galich's drama, capitalism is infinitely bound up in foreign intervention. Class war is a war to liberate the nation.

Alan Bolt, clearly aligned at the time with the Sandinista platform, uses the same rhetorical method when laying out the events of Nicaragua's history in *Banana Republic*. The events of the national history are laid out as a series of class struggles. First, the indigenous people struggle, unsuccessfully, against colonial powers. Then a series of Liberal leaders attempt to bring about reforms in the name of a growing Nicaraguan bourgeoisie against a Conservative aristocracy. However, the aristocracy aligns itself with foreign capitalists. Sandino's unsuccessful fight against the U.S.-backed Conservatives, echoes the struggle to come, and indeed the play leaves off before the 1979 triumph. The audience fills in the information at the end, knowing that the progression of class struggles leads to the popular revolution and national liberation.

If a dramatist aligned with the project of the popular revolution might follow the teleological emplotment of history, as in the case of Bolt and Galich, a writer opposed to revolution might seek a different model. Conservative writers such as Pablo Antonio Cuadra would emplot the prerevolutionary history as a cycle that mirrors the never-ending cycle of Oedipal patricide as outlined in the theories of Sigmund Freud.

8   PABLO ANTONIO CUADRA AND THE CRIMES OF THE BROTHER CLAN

Freud bases his model of political repression and upheaval on the Oedipal urge of the sons to overthrow the domination of the father-king. This model represents the revolution as part of a cycle of patricide and domination. While the brother clan may seek to end domination, their own guilt translates into a series of institutions and laws to keep society in check. In short, the brothers may no longer murder the father (and Freud claims that whether they actually commit murder is unimportant), but civilization is transmitted and renewed through the containment of Oedipal aggression through guilt. Herbert Marcuse takes this model of "progress in domination" further to talk about the revolutionary moment:

> At the societal level, recurrent rebellions and revolutions have been followed by counter-revolutions and restorations. From the slave revolts in the ancient world to the socialist revolution, the struggle of the oppressed has ended in establishing a new, "better" system of domination; progress has taken place through an improving chain of control.[1]

Marcuse goes on to explain that a certain self-defeat is built into the dynamic of revolution and counterrevolution. Those who retain power after those in power have been removed must rationalize the repression of others in the name of preserving the society and liberty, which is only guaranteed by domination.[2] Playwrights who use this model show the revolution as the struggle for power that results in the ultimate corruption of those who take power.

Nicaraguans suffered under a vicious cycle of partisan warfare during the past century and a half. Pablo Antonio Cuadra attempts to examine the civil strife in the years immediately following the resistance by Sandino and the rise of the Somoza family, in his play *Por los caminos van los campesinos* (*Down the Road the Peasants Go*). The play ends, however, looking forward, with a scathing critique of those who would continue the cycle.

Por los caminos van los campesinos

Pablo Antonio Cuadra Cardenal (1912–2002) grew up during the worst of the partisan conflict between the Liberal and Conservative parties. His pedigree put him on the side of the Conservatives in the south, and he lived in Granada off and on during his lifetime. Despite his Conservative leanings, Cuadra admired Sandino, whose historic struggle against U.S. intervention happened during Cuadra's youth. Cuadra was a small, bespectacled, learned man who championed some of the best ideals of modernism: universal brotherhood, faith, and progress. Although he was mostly Conservative, his high ideals usually put him at odds with whoever happened to be in power at the time.

Cuadra's early experiences caused him to be suspicious of politics and politicians, although he never hesitated to give his opinion of any political situation. He ran, for a number of years, the opposition newspaper (opposition during both the Somoza regimes and the Sandinista government) *La Prensa*, in which he promoted Nicaragua's national literature; he wrote scathing political commentary in the paper as well.

When he was not yet twenty years old, Cuadra started the Vanguardia movement with his friends (and distant cousins) José Coronel Urtecho and Joaquín Pasos. The purpose of the group was to develop a uniquely Nicaraguan literary tradition, but ideologically the group leaned toward fascism. Cuadra believed that only a dictatorship could bring peace to the troubled country. In his twenties, Cuadra admired Hitler and Mussolini, and felt that the partisan warfare could only be halted by a strong hand. When Somoza came to power in the 1930s, Cuadra welcomed his leadership.

It was during this time that Cuadra wrote *Por los caminos van los campesinos*, the most famous of his dramatic works. The title comes from Cuadra's poem, his preferred form of creative expression, of the same name:

> Two by two,
> Ten by ten,
> A hundred by a hundred,
> A thousand by a thousand,
> barefoot the peasants go
> with coat and gun.[3]

In the poem, Cuadra expresses his lament at watching the war waste the lives of the people around him. He sees a land emptied of its citizens:

> The farm abandoned,
> the cornfield alone, the bean field burned.
> The bird flying
> about the dumb ear
> and the heart crying
> its naked tear.

From the last stanza comes the title:

> Two by two,
> Ten by ten,
> A hundred by a hundred,
> A thousand by a thousand,
> Down the road the peasants go
> to the civil war![4]

Through this image and the subsequent discourse of the play, Cuadra reveals a rejection of the notion of popular revolution as the answer.

The play begins on the farm of a peasant family. Sebastiano López, his wife, Juana, and their three children live on a farm in uncertain times and in precarious circumstances. Cuadra uses his command of language to describe the farm dwelling, which is personified in the cast of characters: "that is like a mute person, who lives in all of us." The straw hut sits under a tree, like it is "under a green angel," a symbol of Sebastiano's poverty. Cuadra continues:

> Its presence, depending on the time and the light, is like the presence of poverty: humble at times, groomed by peace and its breezes; sorrowful at others. Torn by burning rage: cardinal red. At times ashen, pale, like a temple of misery under the moon. The farm is a character who is glad or cries, who holds in hatred or saves its complaint like an old starving animal.[5]

In the final hours of the morning, the characters gather on the stage.

The middle child of the three, Margarito, enters with his wife, Rosa. As they exchange folk humor, Margarito picks up his guitar and sings:

> The poor man is a disgrace because of his poverty.
> If they see the poor man collapsed already they say that it is for
>   laziness.

If he takes a drink, it is sour and if he does not, it's sweet.
If he brings money he is robbed but if he asks to borrow it they tell him
  that he is shameless.[6]

Cuadra uses the folk songs to comment on the difficult lives of the poor,
who cannot seem to get a break in a world in which they are judged for
their poverty.

The humor quickly turns to the topic of the raging civil war. Margarito
spins his stories into an allegory of the two warring parties:

[T]here was a graying man who had bad tangles with two women: but it turns
out each of the two wanted it her own way. One, who was much younger,
wanted him with black hair. The other, who was much older, wanted him
with white hair. And every day, one removed a little white hair from his
head, the other removed a little black hair from his head. The one, a little
white hair. The other, a little black hair. Until they left him bald![7]

The women, Margarito explains, are the Liberals and Conservatives, who
will leave Nicaragua bald with their fighting.

Sebastiano and Juana are concerned for the future of the farm. Their
lawyer, Fausto Montes, recommended by a friend, has managed to get the
family into trouble with their taxes, and they are in danger of losing the
land. The lawyer has expressed interest in their young daughter, Soledad,
but Sebastiano knows that Fausto is only interested in the land. Juana
convinces him to clear up their business with Fausto and to find another
lawyer. Margarito adds another refrain to his song:

The poor man is a disgrace because of his poverty.
It's useless being clever,
if he finds himself in Court,
even though he is in the right,
between the Judge and the Lawyer,
they leave him without his trousers.[8]

The poor cannot even obtain justice. An encounter with the legal system
usually ends in yet another loss for the *campesino*.

Margarito and Rosa leave on their various errands, but before they can
get far, Soledad returns to tell her parents that soldiers are coming to
conscript men into service in the war against the Liberal rebels. The
Lópezes' younger son, Pancho, runs off to hide. When the soldiers arrive
and ask who lives there, Sebastiano replies, "A poor old man with the

heavy burden of working for these women."[9] But the sergeant wants to know about his sons. Sebastiano tries to say that he has no idea and that his sons take off at the break of day. The soldier knows he is lying: "Denying the Fatherland your sons!" He has already captured Margarito and will not listen to Sebastiano's pleas to leave him to work on the farm.

One of the soldiers notices that the family has pigs and asks whether they can bring one along for the troops. The sergeant stops him, reminding him that there is an order to respect the property of the civilians. The soldiers convince him to ignore the law so that they can have pork tamales, and the pig is conscripted as well. To cheer his father, Margarito tells him he will return a colonel, but Sebastiano tells him war is no joke. Rosa is distraught, but Sebastiano and Juana convince her to follow the regiment so that she can be close to her husband.

In the next scene, the López family goes to a public telephone station in Catarina, a village in the south. They are trying to reach Margarito's regiment in La Paz Centro, a town midway between León and Managua, to find out how Margarito is doing. Five months have passed since his conscription, and Sebastiano notes that Margarito is already a lieutenant. While they are waiting for a connection, Fausto enters the station.

Fausto sees Soledad and wants to talk with her. When Sebastiano and Juana see Fausto, they decide to tell him that they are not going to do business with him anymore. Fausto objects to the idea that another lawyer would profit from his work. Furthermore, the contract that Sebastiano signed ostensibly gives the land to Fausto. The peasants are duped by the legal wrangling of their lawyer. Before the Lópezes can raise an objection, the line rings through to La Paz.

Sebastiano does not tell Margarito about the conversation with the lawyer. Juana asks about Rosa. Margarito scoffs that she is "like a dead fly" to him. She vanished one day, and he thought she was dead. Later he received word that she was running around with a Liberal faction, with another man. Juana urges him to forget her, but Margarito tells them that this is what makes him fight all the more: "They will know well the name of Lieutenant Margarito López!"[10] They start to ask about the conflict, but they are interrupted when Liberal troops overrun the regiment.

The third scene opens with Sebastiano playing Margarito's guitar. Juana, who is working, scolds him: "The World isn't made with songs," to which Sebastiano replies that he is improving it.[11] Here, Cuadra marks the contrast between Sebastiano and Juana, his mestiza wife:

You know that I don't imagine things. I'm not like you. I put my hand to the
music kneading it the way Soledad pets the dog. In order to ease the pass-
ing time. But I don't pretend—[12]

The two talk with the folk wisdom of old *campesinos*. Juana jokes that
she drinks holy water so that she will not stumble over her words. Sebastiano compares the peasant to a tree, dreaming of growth in his youth, not
dreaming at all during the heat of the day, and then dreaming of the sun
of his youth in his old age. As they talk about what may have become of
Margarito, Juana realizes that they may have brought bad luck upon
themselves. Sebastiano had killed a viper inside the hut. The snake had
been nesting in the mouth of the guitar, and so playing the guitar would
bring the curse of the serpent. Sebastiano appeals to the Virgin Mary and
to St. John in a prayer "against the Serpent" in order to ward off the misfortune. Cuadra paints a picturesque scene of pastoral Nicaraguan life,
with religious and superstitious peasants handling adversity in apparently
simple ways.

Pancho enters to announce that Fausto has the papers to seize the land.
There would be nowhere for the family to go unless someone offered
them shelter. To make matters worse, a Liberal faction has arrived to
conscript Pancho. Cuadra makes his disdain for partisan warfare known:

> *First Soldier:* Are you Red or Green [the colors of the Liberal and Conserva-
> tive parties, respectively]?
> *Sebastiano:* At my age colors fade.
> *First Soldier:* We want people for the Revolution!
> *Juana:* We only have this son who is the one that sustains us. We are poor.
> But we can give you the tortillas from our dinner in order to help you out.

The soldiers continue to harass them. They want an answer to the question of their political persuasion when Pancho surprises his father:

> *Fourth Soldier: (Enters. Indicating Pancho and Sebastiano.)* Are they Liberals?
> *First Soldier:* They won't say!
> *Pancho:* If you are looking for people to fight the Government I'm enlisting!
> *Sebastiano: (Surprised and upset.)* Are you going to struggle for a cause that
> isn't yours?[13]

Pancho decides to fight against the Conservative government because he
believes that the Liberals can do something about the corruption that
directly affects his family.

Unfortunately for the new *compañero,* the leader of this faction is none other than the crooked Fausto. Fausto orders the soldiers to take Pancho at gunpoint as a hostage. He tells Sebastiano and Juana not to tell anyone what has happened. The soldiers also take the second pig to eat. The Lópezes are left with one child and half of their already meager livelihood.

In the subsequent scene, the war has ended, and Sebastiano and Juana are trying to get by without their sons. Sebastiano sits outside listening to the birds when Juana returns from her trip to the market. Sebastiano recounts that he must plow the cornfields with the help of a friend's son, and he laments that his own sons would have children now if they were alive. Juana responds, full of news from town. She has just seen an official, who told the townspeople that the U.S. Marines were in Nicaragua to set things right. He had told the Yankee official about the plight of the López family, and the Yankee had agreed to stop by the López farm to see what could be done. Juana has also heard that Fausto had returned to town, and the old couple worries about what that could mean for them. They leave to speak to a family friend about their missing children, leaving Soledad home alone.

Both the Yankee, named Lieutenant Comfort, and the lawyer enter the scene. Comfort tells Fausto that he must comply with the law. When he meets Soledad, however, the lieutenant forgets his purpose and begins to flirt with her. At first he thinks that Soledad is too young for his advances, but Fausto convinces the marine that tropical girls "ripen" early and are fair game. He continues to egg him on: "My dear commander . . . you're beating around the bush. . . . You do not know these people. . . . She is primitive! She needs force. . . . You talk too much! Take her like a man!"[14] Fausto exacts his revenge on the family by inducing the marine to rape Soledad. When Sebastiano returns upon hearing Soledad's screams, he kills the lawyer with his machete. The marine escapes.

In the epilogue, it is several months later, and Sebastiano is on the run, living in the mountains. It is dawn, and Sebastiano sings Cuadra's poem "Por los caminos van los campesinos." Sebastiano recounts how he had to flee and how Juana died from the harshness of their lives as fugitives. He blames everything on the war:

> Son-of-a-bitch war that puts an end to one's desires and brings what one
> curses. . . . It was the War that brought the lawyer, that brought the Yankee, that brought the looting and the slaughter! It was the War that took
> my Pancho, my oldest! That took Margarito! That took Juana! *(He sinks*

like a stone and sits, almost sobbing, and finishes:) The thing that took my girl, Soledad . . . who I loved most . . . *(He hides his face in his hands and cries in silence.)*

Sebastiano does not realize that Soledad has been looking for him. She enters at the end of his speech, and they are reunited.

Sebastiano tells Soledad about going into hiding, but Soledad tells him that the people of their village understood his actions after they heard about the rape. She also tells him that a young man from the town beat up the marine and fled to the mountains. With this news, Sebastiano realizes that a cycle of vengeance has been set in motion.

In an interview with Ramón Layera, Cuadra claims that *Por los caminos van los campesinos* follows faithfully the Nicaraguan history of partisan war and the cycle of vengeance that played out from generation to generation:

> In reality, the main point of *Por los caminos van los campesinos*, with the symmetry of its four scenes, paints a history that I had only to bring to life and harmonize. I want to say that the good thing about this is that it's based on the same sequence of events as our Nicaraguan history. That which the theatrical action of my play tells you in synthesis is the following: in Nicaragua the history has been made of war and its homicidal conception of power. . . . And the result of the war, whatever your ideas and position, is the oppressive relationship between the strong and the weak. Sebastiano, you understand, blames all of his misfortune on the war. And if there is a revolutionary force in this person it is in his break with the dialectic of hate, of vengeance, and the war. His break is complete.[15]

Cuadra's protagonist sets an example by rejecting the cycle of domination and rebellion.

Cuadra offers Augusto Sandino as a very different example from that of his Marxist colleagues. For Cuadra, Sandino did not engage in patricidal revolution, because he conceded his power as soon as his goal of national sovereignty was met:

> The superiority of the heroic sign of Sandino is that he died, not as a warrior, but looking for peace. He offered to surrender his arms as soon as the last Marine left Nicaragua and he kept his promise. The betrayal to his gesture of peace forever dramatizes his message; he struggled against aggression but didn't take the easy way of the dialectic of violence, instead he tried to break it: he arrived to Managua thinking he could lay down the first stone of a new brotherhood of free men.[16]

Cuadra did not write his drama to be about Sandino, but he instead chose a common peasant, Sebastiano, as a stand-in. Sebastiano and his family are caught up in the cyclical partisan violence, but in the end, Sebastiano rejects the cycle when he speaks of his vision for his unborn grandchild and sends his pregnant daughter away:

> *Sebastiano:* That one is going to open his eyes! Let him grow, Soledad! Let him grow strong under the sun and come with his machete to put things in their place! . . . Because he is going to unite everyone, he is going to ring the bells of the church: "Gather together, all you poor," he is going to say to them! . . . "Here there are only Christians working the land of the poor!" Yes! Your son will tell them this![17]

Soledad misunderstands her father and exclaims: "He will be your vengeance, Papa!"[18] This alarms Sebastiano, who realizes that the child must live and grow apart from his family. He must be clean of the blood that stains Sebastiano:

> *Sebastiano: (Trying to convince her.)* I don't have the right to burden the boy with my bad luck! . . . If you stop here he is going to be the son of a coyote, the son of a wounded tiger attacked by gunshots! Do you want that to happen? Do you want him to be born crooked? *(Brief pause.)* Do you want to lose everything that your mother and I dreamed of for each lost child? Take yourself away from here even as my soul departs! . . . he is a child, a clean child, and I am an old man. An old man stained with blood.[19]

Soledad leaves her father, which symbolizes that the cycle will be broken. She leaves the never-ending conflict of partisan warfare and chooses a new life for her son that is free from the continuous destruction of revolution and counterrevolution.

Like Galich, Pablo Antonio Cuadra presents the metaphor of the child to represent *mestizaje*. Cuadra uses the metaphor to demonstrate Nicaragua's history as a violated nation:

> [T]he son of Soledad, who embodies the final hope in the play, is the son of violation. A bastard of the foreigner. But that which I was driving to write through *Por los caminos van los campesinos* was the history of my people, a mestizo people, the fruit of conflict and fusion of races, of conquest, of invasions and interventions—that is to say, of violations and bastardizations since the remote migrations of the indigenous people—because we the Nicaraguans are a nation-bridge in America. I would like to say: whatever will happen to

the Nicaraguans, what will save us, what will create the future, is to purify it with love, to break with the dehumanizing and homicidal dialectic, to forge a new man capable of building Nicaragua from brotherhood and community.[20]

Soledad carries the child of rape. She suffered brutality at the hands of foreigners in the way that Nicaragua suffers the humiliation of foreign intervention. Her rape represents the entire history of invasion and intervention that creates the modern Nicaraguan people.

Cycles of Patricide

The innocence of the child also represents a new start for Cuadra and his protagonist, Sebastiano. Regardless of the hardship the family has suffered or the brutality of the act of rape, Sebastiano pleads with Soledad that she take the child away from the environment of revenge. The mestizo child, a mix of criollo and indigenous, Nicaraguan and gringo blood, represents a new beginning borne out of violence. The colonizing and imperialist forces created the resultant hybridity. According to Cuadra, the mestizo nation must accept its past and use the language and the skills that emerge from such a union to create a new future. Cuadra attempts to relay the moral lesson of turning away from violence even for a people terribly victimized by the brute force of military intervention.

Although the play was written in the 1930s, Cuadra took up this debate again after the Sandinista Revolution of 1979. The play was performed several times and criticized as reactionary:

> From the period of revolutionary struggle against Somoza to after the Triumph, the play has been performed and edited, including a film for television. Nevertheless, some extremist elements have recently attacked it as "reactionary" after it was used as a revolutionary text. I think that this is inevitable: when the partisan violence is reborn, Sebastiano and his philosophy of love are in the way.[21]

In the same way that Cuadra felt that the Conservative coup and subsequent Liberal uprising of 1926–27 were part of a cycle of violence, rather than a class struggle that could have led to a progressive revolution, he also felt that the Sandinistas perpetuated the same repressive domination. He saw the revolution as more of what had come before, another reaction against the old order by the children of those in power.

This model mirrors the Oedipal model of brothers uniting to rise up against the father. When writing about *La noche de los asesinos* (*Night of the Assassins*), by the Cuban writer José Triana (1932–), Diana Taylor suggests the following:

> The biological pattern—parents give birth and identity to children who will rebel against the father in their own struggle to acquire a separate identity— gives birth to a political model. . . . Yet, the biological model simultaneously undermines their revolutionary identity insofar as the circularity seems predetermined—the children, too, will succumb to this natural and biologically necessary fate of being supplanted by their offspring.[22]

The revolutionary Cuban government criticized Triana's work because it ran counter to the simplifying impulse of the theatre of the revolution. Rather than show the progression of events that lead to class struggle and a triumphant break with the past, these plays show children floundering for a way out of the historical cycle of domination, rebellion, and domination.

Taylor suggests that such plays point to a hope of breaking out of this cycle:

> Rather than espouse the party line, these plays warn against the institutionalization of the revolutionary process; they keep urging for new images, new paradigms that will allow this Revolution to go beyond the limits of the possible hitherto explored. The repetition in these plays is not merely the incessant representation of what already exists, but a striving for creation and regeneration.[23]

The characters in the plays suggest an opening through the possibility that they may do it right the next time. The nationalist playwright suggests that the revolution can create itself anew. The dramatist hopes for the revolution to be more than patricide and to become the progression that the party claimed the revolution to be, a way beyond the past and into the future.

Cuadra lays this responsibility for change at the feet of both parties. The Conservatives may seem corrupt when they conscript Margarito and steal a pig, but the Liberals are as malevolent when they take the second son. The U.S. military makes things even worse with their interference. The two groups are equally corrupt in the eyes of the dramatist; but fighting back is not the answer, according to the protagonist, who is already tainted from taking revenge himself.

For Cuadra, the peasants are a microcosm of Nicaraguan life. The Lópezes are pure of heart and simple by nature. They cannot even conceive of the machinations of their wealthy counterpart, Fausto. As his name implies, the learned man has sold his soul and will do anything and employ anyone to secure his gains. In his paternalist view, Cuadra holds his own aristocratic class culpable for the fate of the poor country folk.

Although both Cuadra and Bolt portray a rather monologic view of Nicaragua's revolutionary history, Cuadra differs from Bolt in showing revolution as cycle rather than using Bolt's teleological approach of revolution as logical outcome. They both employ the *campesino* as the everyman, but Cuadra's portrayal comes off as a distant and paternalist plea for a return to a feudal system that protects the simplistic life of the peasants. Bolt, however, attempts to build his pieces from direct, grassroots involvement with rural communities. As Martin notes: "Bolt seeks an alternative to this version of the culture of poverty that is made quaint and that speaks for a people in such a way as to maintain their underdevelopment."[24] Cuadra speaks for the peasant, but with the romantic notion that the underlying economic structure that makes a peasant class does not need to change.

9 ROLANDO STEINER AND THE INVENTION OF TRADITION

Beyond dramatic content, the act of presenting national drama configures the character of the nation and establishes a national tradition. Eric Hobsbawm defines invented tradition as

> a set of practices, normally governed by overtly or tacitly accepted rules and of a ritual or symbolic nature, which seek to inculcate certain values and norms of behaviour by repetition, which automatically implies continuity with the past. In fact, where possible, they normally attempt to establish continuity with a suitable historic past.[1]

This applies to the establishment of a national theatre in a place where little or no national theatrical tradition has existed. Both Pablo Antonio Cuadra and Alan Bolt rediscover a popular theatre during national upheaval on the basis of a forgotten tradition that preceded the forms imitative of Peninsular drama.

Inventing tradition in the name of reviving lost arts constitutes part of the program to establish stability during a crisis of national identity, such as a revolution. Hobsbawm notes that "they are responses to novel situations which take the form of reference to old situations, or which establish their own past by quasi-obligatory repetition."[2] Where old ways are purposely abandoned, such as the rise of a revolutionary regime, new ways are invented that tie the present to a continuing past.

Hobsbawm states that there are three main types of invented tradition:

> a) those establishing or symbolizing social cohesion or the membership of groups, real or artificial communities, b) those establishing or legitimizing institutions, status or relations of authority, and c) those whose main purpose was socialization, the inculcation of beliefs, value systems and conventions of behavior.... [I]t may be regarded that type a) was prevalent, the other

functions being regarded as implicit in or flowing from a sense of identification with a "community" and/or the institutions representing, expressing or symbolizing it such as a "nation."[3]

Cuadra and Bolt both wanted to establish a theatrical tradition that was identifiably Nicaraguan, that Nicaraguans would recognize and affirm.

Cuadra and the Vanguardia attempted to establish a Nicaraguan theatre based in traditions of language and staging. In the initial stages of the Vanguardia movement, Cuadra and his colleagues conducted research into the early theatre of Nicaragua. Cuadra had no interest in the theatre of the recent era. He felt that the plays of the nineteenth and early twentieth centuries were mostly imitative of the drama of the Iberian Peninsula. He and the others "wanted . . . to create a new theatre. But grounded in what had come before; with Nicaraguan roots."[4] The Vanguardia theatre would be a break with the recent trend of work inspired by European forms.

The mixing of languages and the play of words marks the early colonial drama, and, according to Cuadra, offers a space to subvert colonial power. For the Vanguardia it was a matter of national redefinition. José Joaquín Pasos (1914–1947) and José Coronel Urtecho (1906–1994) wrote *Chinfonía burguesa (Bourgeois Symphony)* as a language experiment. Carlos Solórzano suggests that the central character of Don Chombón represents a modern-day Güegüence.[5] However, more important, Vicky Unruh suggests:

> In Latin America, the preoccupation with language was often recast around questions of national or regional linguistic autonomy, and the dual search for modernity and cultural identity was defined in specifically linguistic terms.[6]

The play of language became a central theme in the nationalist work of the Vanguardia artists, as they believed it had been for the creators of *El Güegüence.*

Cuadra placed equal importance on the theatrical form and its staging. In *Por los caminos van los campesinos,* Cuadra borrowed from the popular street theatre of Nicaragua. The introduction to the 1986 edition of Cuadra's play states that the work

> was written with the intention to be represented as "street theatre" in the alleys and streets of the cities and towns, in order to bring to the people a message of rebellion against politics as usual.[7]

Cuadra says in the Layera interview that each act could be staged in a different part of the plaza, and the singing and music could happen in the street, much in the spirit of *El Güegüence*. He felt that both the mobility of the staging and the use of the vernacular language and popular songs made it essentially Nicaraguan theatre.[8]

This type of agitprop theatre, with its episodic structure, character types, and mix of performance genres, has caused some scholars to classify his work as Brechtian,

> incorporating into the text popular refrains, slogans, and songs, with surprising and creative spontaneity, . . . characters are not just psychological beings in themselves, but are "types" so that the internal action manifests in an increasing and poetic progression.[9]

Cuadra, however, refutes the notion that he is at all influenced by what was going on in Europe. He believed he was calling for something uniquely Nicaraguan:

> I wasn't familiar with Brecht. I learned about him much later. I was familiar a little with the work of Lorca [and with Rafael Alberti]. . . . And it is still astonishing to us how we, without knowing we had, sought those same popular sources and those same games and those playful forms in the theatre. I must clarify, nevertheless, that I did not do this consciously in *Por los caminos van los campesinos*. This work had a very local and very intimate origin within the country. The popular street theatre inspired me in such a way that, if you think about *Por los caminos van los campesinos*, their acts or scenes are done so that each section has a kind of independence and particular mobility.[10]

Cuadra used his research to establish a new form of Nicaraguan theatre, supposedly based in a long tradition. He called for theatre companies to be started in every town's existing theatres or town squares. Although he said that artists should use these performance spaces to present drama and performance of all kinds, the Vanguardia focused on the development of drama based in Cuadra's folk drama format.[11]

Alan Bolt used similar forms when he formed the Nixtayolero group in 1980. Bolt and Cuadra share similar elements with local language, protagonists who are both clever and simple, and a street form that was mobile and accessible. Bolt, in the introduction to *Banana Republic* states:

> With *Banana Republic* we hope to begin anew a process of recuperation of the forms that our people have used in the traditional performances, from

El Güegüense and the Indians to the circus of Firuliche. It has been said insistently that there is no tradition of theatre in Nicaragua, and I am in disagreement and think that there is a rich scenic and theatrical tradition. And I think that when they negate our theatrical tradition, they see our reality, as Martí said: through North American glasses. In the struggle against every form of oppression, for the development of a revolutionary culture, our duty is to recover the forms created by our people and engage with the future that we have all created.[12]

Bolt argues that the theatrical tradition that his company helped establish has always existed. He charges that anyone who disagrees with his claim of continuity stands on the side of U.S. imperialists who deny a Nicaraguan culture.

Cuadra and the Vanguardia also advanced the idea for a national theatre and created drama as part of a movement separate from the Nicaraguan government; to a large degree, their lack of success can be traced to the failure of the movement to coincide with the existing power structures. Somoza later censured Cuadra and his colleagues. *Por los caminos van los campesinos* fits Hobsbawm's first and third types of invented tradition, in that it establishes social cohesion and inculcates beliefs and values. However, the work did not support or legitimate the current regime. Bolt, however, created a group and a work that fit in with the Sandinista program of popular art for political education. *Banana Republic,* then, fits all of Hobsbawm's categories.

Sites of Memory

Hobsbawm and Ranger, in *The Invention of Tradition,* point to a crisis of memory. Rather, in the sense that traditions are invented when old ones are abandoned, sites of memory are constructed to replace actual lived memory. This holds particular relevance for the so-called third world as groups move from colonized traditional societies into nations with a national history. As Richard Terdiman comments on Hobsbawm:

> Invented traditions establish or symbolize the cohesion of such polities, whose existence, however artificial, becomes internalized within the memories of those subjected to it as if it were a fact beyond change and independent of memory.[13]

The memorialization of the national history reflects an erasure of the memory of those events and a negation of the fact that this nation and this history are recent constructs.

Along with Terdiman, Pierre Nora places this phenomenon within the modern era, an era marked by what Nora calls the "acceleration of history."[14] Nora believes this has particular relevance for the developing countries because "independence has swept into history societies newly awakened from their ethnological slumbers by colonial violation."[15] For my purposes, this holds particularly true for Nicaragua and Guatemala, because they have struggled to free themselves from economic domination by the United States.

As revolution creates a rupture in the national history, stories of the revolution and the events leading up to it take the form of collective memory. In Nicaragua, dramatists used stories of Augusto Sandino, because he was considered the father of the 1979 revolution. Sandino grew in importance also as stories of his struggles began to slip from lived memory.

La noche de Wiwilí and Official Memory

Most scholars of Nicaraguan theatre associate Rolando Steiner (1936–1987) with the experimental theatre of the 1960s, along with Alberto Ycaza (1945–2002) and José de Jesús Martínez (1929–1991). Steiner's plays tend to explore heterosexual relationships and the difficulty that men have relating to women. In *Judit* (1957), for instance, the main character, Julián Rojas, ends up killing his wife when he attempts to destroy an imaginary woman. In Steiner's play *La puerta* (*The Door*) (1966), a man comes home to find that he cannot get through his front door. His key does not work in the lock. His wife is similarly trapped on the other side. As they converse through the door, all the failings of their marriage come to light.

Steiner took an interest in helping Cuadra develop a canon of Nicaraguan literature. In the 1960s he was coeditor with Cuadra of *El pez y la serpiente* (*The Fish and the Serpent*), a Central American cultural review founded by Cuadra. Steiner's early plays received international recognition, and *La puerta* was staged at the 1968 Olympics in Mexico City.[16] Steiner's later plays, written after the 1979 revolution, are the ones that take up the issue of national history.

In 1982 Steiner published his exceedingly short play *La noche de Wiwilí* (*The Night of Wiwilí*) in the *Boletín nicaragüense de bibliografía y documentación* (Nicaraguan Bulletin of Bibliography and Documentation), a cultural review put out by the Banco Central de Nicaragua. The play is based on the bombardment of the village of Wiwilí by a U.S. pilot after Sandino's assassination in 1934. In the play, a group of women lament that their settlement has been attacked, and they relate the events that lead to the bombing. The scenes give a flashback historical account of Sandino's betrayal by Somoza.

La noche de Wiwilí begins in the immediate aftermath of the bombardment. Seven women shout curses at the bombardier, who has just devastated their village. They wonder at the sanity of a person who would bomb defenseless women and children: "Why did they do this to us? What harm were we doing to them?"[17] One woman reasons that it must be because their men fought with Sandino during the uprising. Knowing that Sandino has just signed the peace accord, another woman says bitterly: "This is what we get for believing in peace."[18] Smoke and flames transition the scene to the moment when the men sign the accord.

During the signing, Sandino gives a stirring speech, recounting the many years that he and his handful of men starved and suffered together for the struggle. He attributes their success to their unshakable faith and to the will of God. He signs the accord, he says, without conditions, because he wants to live in peace. The admiring crowd cheers him on. President Sacasa nervously accepts Sandino's capitulation. The scene shifts back to the mourning women, who note that in addition to their personal loss, no one has heard anything of Sandino in nine days. One woman suggests that maybe he has been killed as well. The women worry that there is no one left to defend them.

The next scene shows a hypothetical meeting between Somoza, then a general of the National Guard, and Arthur Lane, the U.S. ambassador to Nicaragua. Somoza paces around, fuming at the new accord between Sacasa and Sandino. He and Lane both agree that they want Sandino out of the north, where Sandino has asked that he be given a district for his faction. Somoza bristles at the idea: "This is an insult for the National Guard, and an intolerable insult for me. To put to my men under the orders of Sandino, in the most extensive region of the country."[19] For Lane, removing Sandino will clear the way for U.S. imperialism. Somoza prefers that no one stand in the way of his own ambitions and will gladly remove Sandino with the help of the United States. The two men conspire to wipe out the settlement at Wiwilí. Although Lane says that he should not become involved directly in these kinds of machinations, he promises to support Somoza's actions and even gives him the name of a fighter pilot who might prove to be useful.

As Somoza heads off into the night, the headlights of a car mark the beginning of the next scene. An official stops the car, which carries Sandino and his father, Don Gregorio. Minister Salvatierra and two officers ride with them as well. The official tells them that they are detained by order of General Somoza, which confuses Sandino: "Just three nights ago General Somoza visited me and embraced me as a sign of harmony. Call General Somoza!"[20] The official's phone call confirms Somoza's orders. He tells Salvatierra and Don Gregorio to stay put, and he leads Sandino and his generals away. Hoping that they are all just prisoners, Salvatierra tells Don Gregorio that they will call on Sacasa the next day to straighten everything out. In the next minute, they hear gunshots, and they know that Sandino is dead.

Ambassador Lane appears and offers presidential protection to Salvatierra and Don Gregorio. The two men stand in shock and ask for Sandino. Lane tells them, coldly, "Although the President and General Somoza assure me that they aren't informed about what has happened to him, I have reason to think that General Sandino has been killed."[21] Everyone washes their hands of the murder.

The women enter again and wonder what their fate will be now that the men are gone. As one woman notes: "We could stay on this road forever. No one misses us. Now we are like stones or trees, that don't move, because we have nowhere to go. I could grow old and die sitting here!"[22] Ultimately, the women reject the idea of immobility. One woman hears voices. They are the voices of Sandino and the other men calling to them. They agree to follow the men. They lift "a beautiful red and black flag,"[23] the flag of the Sandinistas, overhead and march offstage.

At first glance, the play seems to be a flat piece of nationalist propaganda. It takes a well-known story from history and ties it to the nationalist project. However, Steiner's play is more interesting for what it erases than for what it highlights. The scene in which Somoza's men detain Sandino's car comes directly from an account given by a guardsman who was on the scene.[24] The event passes from memory and is memorialized through Steiner's drama. The fact that Steiner takes it from an eyewitness account makes the events of the play seem indisputable, a totalization that wipes out individual memory and creates a universal history.

The revolutionary regime has the primary task of stabilization, which it accomplishes by taking the collective and unifying it under singular signs. Memorialization takes the individual understanding of past events and harmonizes them with the national will to the future. The audience/citizens of the nation can collectively affirm this erasure of memory and thereby acknowledge a certain legitimacy to the new state, but not because they are so willing to forget. Such an affirmation allows for temporal boundaries carved out by plumbing past events to write a national history and to make the current character of the nation seem coherent and continuous in the shifting landscape.

10 Interweavings, Hybrid Identities, and Contested Narratives

> The very concept of homogenous national cultures, the
> consensual or contiguous transmission of historical traditions,
> or "organic" ethnic communities—*as the grounds of cultural
> comparativism*—are in a profound process of redefinition. The
> hideous extremity of Serbian nationalism proves that the very
> idea of a pure, "ethnically cleansed" national identity can only
> be achieved through the death, literal and figurative, of the
> complex interweavings of history, and the culturally contin-
> gent borderlines of modern nationhood. This side of the
> psychosis of patriotic fervour, I like to think, there is over-
> whelming evidence of a more transnational and translational
> sense of the hybridity of imagined communities.
> —Homi K. Bhabha, *The Location of Culture*

I have argued that the nation exists between fact and imagination, that
the historical and geographical facts of the nation are signs that are deployed in the course of the performance of the nation. The performance
strives to resolve the tension between the ruptures of history, most notably ruptures of national revolution, and the continuity required for
legitimation.

In the case of the statue that I discussed at the beginning of this book,
Somoza rode on horseback in the plaza of the Palacio Nacional through
much of this century as a symbol of the "last marine," Nicaragua under
the hand of the strongman. At the break of the 1979 revolution, the remaining fragment of the statue carried a double meaning. Popular feeling toward the Somoza dynasty left the sign where Somoza placed it with
his original signification still visible under the new sign of Sandinista
victory. The painters of the León mural added the fragment to the line
of Nicaraguan history, making historical sense of the demise of the statue

and the choice to leave it in the plaza. The new president after the 1990 UNO victory would later erase it.

The plaza in Managua provided a public sphere for the affirmation of the sign of the statue until the fragment was moved recently. The site of the mural in León provides that site of affirmation today. Daily, people pass this representation, the palimpsest of signification only adding to the richness of the meaning. The continuity of the dictator on horseback follows through even the fear of its erasure, existing in dynamic tension with the myriad meanings the statue has presented.

In the same public way, the success of national drama lies within its ability to call together an audience who can recognize themselves and one another as citizens. They recognize themselves in the action of the play, and they recognize one another as actors in the ritual of affirming the nation. The ritual finds its liminality in the fact that each performance, in this string, makes the nation anew, altered, but with the appearance of having been merely restored. The national drama ultimately fails because it attempts to fix something that proves all too fluid, and the repeat performances belie its fluidity. Thus, we run up against the crisis of the performance of the nation.

If we place the nation between geographical and historical fact, on the one hand, and the imagination of both those who count themselves as its citizens and those who look from the outside, on the other hand, then we are left to ask where the nation will reside as we move from the modern era into the postmodern one. Bhabha suggests that groups and communities on the margins, such as in Nicaragua and Guatemala, have existed "otherwise than modernity," as he theorizes on the location of culture. Postmodernist discourse, then, is necessarily postcolonial, because the center finds itself always already decentered, and those on the margins find their voice, "the authentication of histories of exploitation and the evolution of strategies of resistance."[1]

Bhabha speaks of the "unhomeliness" of the postcolonial subject, the "condition of the extra-territorial and cross-cultural initiations."[2] Where Fanon saw both the necessity of turning away from the corpses of the past and the need for a culture that emerges from the struggle of decolonization, Bhabha takes up the notion that the processes of colonization, imperialism, migration, and exile have created a sense of strangeness about the once familiar.

In Guatemala the struggle for national identity turned violent in the 1980s, with the forced relocation of mostly indigenous people from their villages to "model hamlets," a move that wrenched a populace from historical context and created an alienated generation to be inscribed by the power of the center. Resistance took the form of fractured rebel groups, the conflict unearthing myriad protest voices. Gerald Martin reveals the inextricable link formed between Miguel Ángel Asturias and his indigenous alter ego in the introduction to his translation of *Hombres de maíz,* when he points out that Asturias's son Rodrigo had a prominent role in Organización Revolucionaria del Pueblo en Armas (Revolutionary Organization of People in Arms). In a twist of history, people call Rodrigo Gaspar Ilóm, the legendary figure who occupies the first part of Asturias's *Hombres de maíz.*[3]

For present-day Nicaragua, the struggle for national sovereignty has led to a solidarity with groups and sister-city organizations around the world. I was in Corinto in 1989 with the Portland–Corinto Sister City Association on the Benjamin Linder Construction Brigade, named for the young man from Portland who was murdered by the Contras in 1987 while helping to build a hydroelectric dam for the village of El Cuá. Two other such brigades were there, one from Bremen, West Germany, and the other from Liverpool, England. We met with a group of musicians in Corinto who had called themselves Arena and were just changing their name to Los Beatles.

We met with several groups of people in different parts of the Pacific region, from Masaya to Matagalpa. We met with Alan Bolt, who said of the United States that he was surprised how little theatre people knew of the world, and we met with women from the Ocho de Marzo women's collective in Managua. Whereas Bolt has become something of a celebrity in the study of Latin American theatre, Ocho de Marzo struggles just to provide basic services to women and performs theatre on a shoestring in the poorest of neighborhoods in Managua. Ocho de Marzo builds the nation on a microlevel and networks with organizations across national borders.

Like Nixtayolero, Ocho de Marzo began as part of the postrevolutionary culture and literacy campaigns under the auspices of the Ministry of Culture. It continues to represent a growing movement of theatre workers who attempt to initiate change locally. Rather than a call for a "national" theatre, as Cuadra has suggested, some artists turn to the present moment to create the national culture. As Fanon notes:

> The artist who has decided to illustrate the truths of the nation turns paradoxically toward the past and away from actual events. What he ultimately

intends to embrace are in fact the castoffs of thought, its shells and corpses, a knowledge which has been stabilized once and for all. But the native intellectual who wishes to create an authentic work of art must realize that the truths of a nation are in the first place its realities. He must go on until he has found the seething pot out of which the learning of the future will emerge.[4]

Ocho de Marzo creates a national culture by empowering women to participate in creating their own reality. They attempt to change the dynamics of oppression created by colonialism and the subsequent neocolonial relationship with economic powers of the center.

Loren Kruger observes this dynamic in her essay on postcolonial theatre in South Africa:

The significance of this local theatre for a theatre with national aspirations lies in its attempt to adumbrate an alternative public sphere, in which participants may realize their potential agency, in which subjunctive action might entertain direct action without immediately enforcing it. It makes the case for the radical decentralization that Fanon sees as the necessary step if national consciousness-raising is to be democratic rather than a nationalist variant of colonial paternalism.[5]

The theatre of Ocho de Marzo is the arena of the nation, being created at the local level for small resistances which form part of a larger web of social change. The key to Ocho de Marzo's role in nation building lies within the changing roles for women in the postrevolutionary culture.

Women and the Revolution

> We make up more than half the population, and without us
> there would have been no revolution.
> —Magda Henriques, director of international
> relations for the Luisa Amanda Espinoza
> Association of Nicaraguan Women (AMNLAE)

Women made up a large percentage of the Sandinista military force during the revolution against the Somoza regime. The involvement of women in revolutionary activity can often advance women's rights. However, it is frequently the case that as war subsides, women are demobilized and relegated to the traditional position of wife and mother:

Unless women are politically self-conscious about what they want to gain from their participation in the revolution's military effort, they are likely to be demobilised as part of the process of creating both a new public order and a new state military organisation. Eventually, even their political leverage as liberation army veterans may dissolve.[6]

Although Nicaraguan women were indeed demobilized, they did not lose their institutional cohesiveness. The AMNLAE group was already in place when the victory of the revolution was ensured.

By tying its objectives to the project of the revolution, AMNLEA succeeded in securing the gains of women. Its advancement of the women's agenda through legislature brought about programs to educate and provide health care to rural and urban women. In Managua, the Ocho de Marzo health collective began to experiment with theatrical presentations for outreach purposes. Faced with counseling many women who would not report domestic violence, the women of Ocho de Marzo devised a drama to address the issue. They took the performance out into the neighborhoods and performed in community centers, houses, and in the street.

In the performance, a drunk man comes home and proceeds to escalate his abuse as his wife continually fails to meet his impossible demands. When she fails to meet them, he lashes out at her and leaves. The neighbor urges her to call the police. The neighbor finally convinces the woman that she has a right to have her husband arrested and that she must exercise that right.

This simple skit received positive responses, but within a year, the group had turned over. Rosa Estela Valle Chavarria began to write longer scenarios. The improvisations became set dialogue and stage action. Valle Chavarria wanted to address three issues: the role of women in society, women's health care, and domestic violence. In the early 1990s, the group performed three plays, which I saw when the group traveled to Madison, Wisconsin, in 1993. The protagonists are faced with drunk and absent husbands, unsupportive parents, women with no sense of feminist solidarity, and misinformation.

The first play, *Woman or Mother?*, follows the character Elena from marriage to political awareness. In between, Elena is bombarded with the expectations of others: the church, her parents, and her husband. In the marriage ceremony, the priest spells out how he expects the woman to be submissive and obedient. Society also expects her to have as many children as possible. Elena's husband mistreats Elena, using her sexually and abandoning her when she becomes pregnant. He returns only to ask for money when he is broke. Elena finally refuses to take him back. Although she must then survive as a single mother, she makes a decision to work for women's rights.

The second play the group performed, *The Story of Young Love*, examines the lack of health and sexuality information available to young Nicaraguan women. It also focuses on the fact that abortion is not legal and is difficult to obtain. In the play, neither parent will talk with their daughter, Andrellita, about her sexuality. When Andrellita becomes pregnant at the age of fifteen, her mother decides that Andrellita must have an illegal abortion so that the father does not find out. If he knew, he would throw Andrellita out of the house. The abortion results in serious injury to Andrellita, and she must be taken to the hospital. After Andrellita dies, the family breaks up. Ocho de Marzo used the play to help the audience explore where the blame lay for the girl's death.

The third play, *Confronting Abuse*, contains many of the same elements as the 1989 skit I saw performed on domestic violence. In the play, the abusive husband, Pinpano, pressures his wife, Pepa, to have another child. They have six daughters, but he wants a boy, even though he cannot support the large family. Pepa considers finding a job, but she cannot imagine how she would work outside the home with everything else she has to do. She begins reciting a monologue of her daily schedule. As she speaks, she moves back and forth, trying to get some of her work done. Her delivery becomes more rapid, as do her movements, until she is speaking and moving at a comic speed:

> I get up in the morning at 5A.M., make breakfast, bathe the children, get them ready for school, feed them, take them to school, on my way home I do the shopping, once I get home I get lunch ready and do the wash, I take Pinpano his lunch, I pick up the children from school, I wash the lunch dishes, clean the house, change the children's clothes, sew, prepare dinner, serve dinner, wash the dishes, boil the food for the next day's meals . . . I iron while I tell the children bedtime stories about how they should behave themselves like young ladies and be thankful for what Pinpano gives them.[7]

Pepa collapses after her delivery, causing roars of laughter and acknowledgement from the audience. The list represents the load of responsibilities that many women in Nicaragua face. Pepa demonstrates not only the ways she must fulfill the role of wife and mother but also the ways she must perpetuate the cycle of sexism as she passes on this role to her six daughters.

Pepa works hard to maintain the household, but she receives no support from the men in her life. She has no value in Nicaraguan society.

Pinpano is abusive when he comes in after drinking with his friend. This time, the female neighbor, Temcha, instead of urging her to call the police, reinforces Nicaraguan gender roles by always siding with the men. Pepa grows tired of being unappreciated, and she vows to leave her situation so that she can find herself.

The Ocho de Marzo group members lack resources for their productions, and they employ techniques such as using masks, shifting to inner voices or dreams, and using objects not worn on an actor to suggest another character. This makes for an original theatrical form that has grown largely out of necessity. These techniques move the presentations away from a realism that supports mimesis and toward a form that turns silence into discourse and spurs the creation of local and attainable tactical positions. Rather than ask the women in the audience to identify with the characters, the actors hold up the characters as subjects for critical debate.

Michel Foucault's definition of power as something polyvalent can help illuminate the way the women achieve a dialogic presentation. It can also provide an understanding of how the work of small, grassroots organizations such as Ocho de Marzo can build the nation at the local level. In *The History of Sexuality,* Foucault describes power as "the moving substrate of force relations which, by virtue of their inequality, constantly engender states of power, . . . local and unstable."[8]

Discourse, Foucault suggests, "can be both an instrument and effect of power, but also a hindrance, a stumbling block, a point of resistance and a starting point for an opposing strategy."[9] AMNLAE did not always win in the debate over the role of women in the defense of the revolution, but it found the opening in which the debate could take place. So, too, Ocho de Marzo cannot eradicate sexism and domestic violence from its district; the group's talent lies in laying bare the power relationships and the sexist discourse that perpetuate ignorance and violence. The group was able to recognize the power shifts created by both the revolution and AMNLAE and find the resulting new tactical positions. This enabled the group to secure programs and funding in order to keep issues of importance to women in the public discourse.

I cannot speak to the motivations behind the staging choices that Ocho de Marzo makes. Valle Chavarria told a group at the University of Wisconsin–Madison in 1993 that the use of masks to play multiple roles came out of necessity. They only had three actors and several characters that they wanted to show. The theatrical devices are also not uncommon to presentations in Nicaragua. But the results of those choices, I believe, are ultimately empowering.

At one point in the production, masks are held out, one or several at a time, from behind a screen. They speak to the protagonist as they appear. These disembodied masks represent the unending demands placed on the woman in the home, by her children, her husband, her parents. She becomes exhausted from trying to be what the voices want her to be. The masks represent social forces more than they represent individuals, and they offer an opening for an examination of those forces.

The actors assume many characters, creating different institutional constellations, such as the family or the church. When assuming a new role, an actor puts on a mask, and it is clear that she puts on the power accorded to the character associated with that mask. Power is shown as performance and not an embodiment. The women watching the performance can see that the power of the characters is not natural or inherent but performed. In the opening scene of the first play, as Elena is getting married, one woman dons the mask and robe of the priest. She speaks a few words of the marriage ceremony in which the woman is told to obey her husband and have many children, and then the priest makes some nonsense sounds to the effect of "blah, blah, blah." The audience at the University of Wisconsin laughed uproariously at the lampooning of church power. The actor does not embody the character but offers a representation as a point of criticism.

I think that the way that the group staged works in the past, ending at identification with a desired solution tagged on, did not create the kind of dialogue the women of the collective wanted. The current staging methods Ocho de Marzo employs engage the women who see the plays and reveal the workings of power so that they can speak critically about them. Foucault suggests that discourse can merely reinforce the dominant discourse or it can alter it. There is a difference between identification and action.

The dramatic presentations of Ocho de Marzo take into account the varied experiences of the women from different neighborhoods. Moving beyond the role play of the consciousness-raising workshops of the other groups, the theatre group moves the issues out of the building and into the realm of public discourse. The plays are part of an ongoing dialogue between the collective and the local women:

> The group writes and produces all of its own plays based on their own experience and the experiences of the women with whom they work. They

adapt each performance to fit the needs of the audience. At the end of the performance, the actors invite the audience to discuss the play and give their reactions and suggestions. The group then takes these suggestions to improve their plays.[10]

The women of Ocho de Marzo use the experiences of the women in the audience to write their plays, but it is important to note that these are also the experiences of the organizers. These are not professional actors, outsiders to the neighborhood. These are women who come from the kinds of circumstances that they seek to change. The fact that they incorporate the feedback from the audience also demonstrates that the women of the collective wish to remain close to their constituency.

The work of Ocho de Marzo constitutes nation building from the grass roots, the "low" culture. The women of the collective took a political opening created by the participation of women in the revolution and paved the way to a new vision of a Nicaragua that included women in all aspects of national life. Initially, this approach fit the Sandinista program of putting the task of nation building in the hands of the people. Even when the Sandinistas became the high culture, Ocho de Marzo struggled to remain close to the women it served.

In general, the struggle for signification in the national culture involves the negotiation of elements in the high culture. Those who have agency in the formation of national culture may appropriate "the people" to that end. Cuadra appropriated the *campesino;* Asturias, the indigenous. The strongest force of nation building remains a top-down dynamic. This explains why so few women dramatists occupy the pages of this book. The 1979 Sandinista Revolution and the emphasis on Nicaraguan culture created a proliferation of grassroots cultural activity. Rather than the national culture emerging from the clash of high cultures in a struggle for hegemony, much of the revolutionary culture initially emerged from the ground up. At the revolutionary moment, women took part in defining the national culture, and, moreover, they helped change what it means to be a woman in Nicaragua.

Around the time the Sandinistas lost the general election in 1990 to the U.S.-backed coalition of UNO, the women of the Ocho de Marzo collective began to feel the need to be independent from the Sandinista organization. Even as participation in the revolution helped create an opening for the existence of feminist organizations, the policies and politics of the revolution restrained the collectives. As Bertha Inéz Cabrales said in an interview with Julie Andersen: "The priority for AMNLAE is class struggle, class conflict. They would feel that through class struggle they would resolve the whole issue of subordination of women."[11] The party took the concerns of the women as secondary to their own concerns, at the same time appropriating the image of the Nicaraguan woman as a powerful symbol of revolutionary patriotism. As a nationalist performance by the high culture, the revolution began to evolve into a "passive" one, in which the concerns of the people, in this case women, would be represented but in which the people would not have direct agency.[12]

According to Andersen, the break with the official party was met with resistance. The leaders of AMNLAE interpreted the desire of the collective leaders to put the concerns of women before party goals as traitorous and dangerous to both the revolution and the objectives of AMNLAE. For the party, losing the women meant facing the lack of the consistent national identity for which the party claimed to be the ultimate representation.

If the group represents, on the one hand, a desire to change the dynamics of creating national culture, the group represents, on the other hand, the transnational redefinition of the idea of nation. The collective receives support from groups in Italy, Germany, Switzerland, Canada, Spain, and the United States. It has come to the United States several times through the auspices of the Wisconsin Coordinating Council on Nicaragua to tour women's shelters and to talk with various groups committed to issues of abortion rights, violence against women, and other gender-equity issues. The dynamic of solidarity with women around the world creates a unique tension between the global and the local, and it shapes the ways in which the women approach the role that women play in creating the nation.

The devastation of Hurricane Mitch, the embezzlement of government funds by Arnoldo Alemán, and the recent global economic crisis have left Nicaragua in dire financial need. It has been an increasing struggle for the women of the collectives to find the resources to do their work and to meet their objectives. The negotiation between the margins and the center becomes even more tense. Men are being laid off more often, feeling frustration that they may take out on the women in their lives. Clinics and women's centers are also receiving less funding. But Ocho de Marzo continues, and even more theatre groups form. The women show their resilience, taking every break in the ground as an opportunity to build.

Learning to Curse and Border Performance

In the same way that small groups activate resistance and build the nation on the microlevel, the transnational shifts create imagined communities that, in the words of Bhabha, "deploy their cultural hybridity of their borderline conditions."[13] Nicaraguans and Guatemalans both live as refugees in the United States and elsewhere, creating national communities in southern Florida, New York, and the Southwest. The slippage created by migration and exile leads to what Gómez-Peña calls a "border experience":

> The colonized cultures are sliding into the space of the colonizer, and in doing so, they are redefining its borders and its culture. The First and Third Worlds have mutually penetrated one another. The two Americas are totally intertwined. . . . Whenever and wherever two or more cultures meet—peacefully or violently—there is a border experience.[14]

This border experience challenges dominant culture notions of a unified developing and developed society or a singular Nicaraguan, or Guatemalan, or U.S. culture. Gómez-Peña's vision is one in which the two sides of the north and south dichotomy blur with and redefine the other.

Specifically, Gómez-Peña uses the blending of languages —Spanish, Nahuatl, English—to slip along the surface of culture. In much the same way, Cuadra appreciated *El Güegüence* for its subversive blending of Nahuatl and Spanish, and Galich employs a specific Guatemalan dialect that sometimes contains words spelled in Spanish to be pronounced in English.

In the same way that nationalists cannot turn to the dead relics of the past to create a national culture, as Fanon suggests, there is no turning back to a dead language.[15] If culture resides in the interstices of language, then the living "mulatto" language of Derek Walcott or the subversive language of *El Güegüence* hold the key to the postcolonial nation.[16] The Cuban writer Roberto Fernández Retamar reminds us of this when he summons up the figure of Caliban, the colonized who has learned the master's language in order to curse:

> Our symbol then is not Ariel, as Rodó thought, but rather Caliban. This is something that we, the *mestizo* inhabitants of these same isles where Caliban lived, see with particular clarity: Prospero invaded the islands, killed our ancestors, enslaved Caliban, and taught him his language to make himself understood. What else can Caliban do but use that same language—today he has no other—to curse him, to wish that the "red plague" would fall on

him? I know no other metaphor more expressive of our cultural situation, of our reality.[17]

The national culture, altered by colonialism and imperialist exploitation, finds its voice in the new language to assert itself. Bhabha finds expressed in Derek Walcott's poem "Sainte Lucie" the "possession of a space through the power of naming."[18] He explains:

> [In language,] in a specifically postcolonial performance of reinscription, the focus shifts from the nominalism of imperialism to the emergence of another sign of agency and identity. It signifies the destiny of culture as a site, not simply of subversion and transgression, but one that prefigures a kind of solidarity between ethnicities that meet in the tryst of colonial history.[19]

The African in the poem watches while the world is named by the colonizer but then turns around and alters the pronunciation and the inflection, thereby altering the language. As does the child born to Soledad in *Por los caminos van los campesinos,* the hybridity of cultures brings the future of the postcolonial nation. Whereas Cuadra's Sebastiano urges Soledad, for the sake of peace, to accept the violence of her violation and move beyond it, Walcott's slave and Fernández Retamar's Caliban take what they are given, reclaim it, and use it to curse.

The Battle over Signification: *El Güegüence*

Cuadra's favorite trickster, El Güegüence, is called before the governor to pay his taxes. The old man speaks a mixture of Nahuatl and Spanish, and his speech is full of double meanings. Güegüence dupes the greedy governor into marrying his daughter to one of Güegüence's sons. They throw a party to celebrate and are carried through the town by the black mules who are present throughout.

This folk dance is still performed in Diriamba, said to be the birthplace of the story. Diriamba is also said to be the birthplace of Diriangén, the indigenous man who successfully routed the Spanish after an ambush and resisted them for six years. The song "Nicaragua, Nicaragüita" states that Nicaragua is fed by Diriangén's blessed blood, in a gesture that appropriates him as the father of the mestizo nation. This year at the Festival of St. Sebastian, the festivities were officially titled "El Güegüence, Father of Humanity." Bayardo Rodríguez, of the Institute of Culture, hopes to have UNESCO classify the work as a national treasure. Nicaraguans are quick to point to this work as the first drama and to the character of the trickster as part of the national persona.

When Irene López staged the work in Managua this year, she stated that *El Güegüense* "is a piece where drama, comedy, tragedy, satire, trickery, and ridicule are joined to protest against the personalities accused of bad government and corruption."[20] The figure of the trickster is viewed as the mestizo spirit who resists colonial rule, and, by extension, imperialism and corrupt government. Polanco adds, as he loosely quotes Cuadra, that the Nicaraguan is, by extension,

> happy, untrustworthy, a liar, a vagabond, a braggart, a satirist, ironic, a master of double-speak, protestor of taxes that drain the piggy bank, deaf person by convenience, sharp with words and with his false deafness (mainly when they want money from him), and malicious. These characteristics are in the Güegüence that, "as it emerged in the initial moment of our cultural mestizaje, summarizes, in caricaturesque and satirical form, all the characteristics that we have coming down to us in Nicaraguan writing." [Cuadra] argues in convincing form that the Güegüence represents the prototype of the Nica, and how he behaves through his adventures, ruses, within social conditions and socio-political relations, [Güegüence] is an x-ray of the personality of the Nicaraguan being.[21]

In July 2000, *The Economist,* in a story recounting Vicente Fox's surprising victory in Mexico, referred to something they called the "Nicaragua Effect." According to the story, Fox's upset over Francisco Labastida

> baffled the many pollsters who had predicted a narrow PRI [Partido Revolucionario Institucional] win. In the 1990 [Nicaraguan] election which ejected the Sandinistas, . . . many voters told pollsters they were undecided right up until the end, then apparently plumped for the opposition.[22]

The Nicaragua effect, according to Latin American political analysts, involves people telling you they plan to do one thing, when they plan to do something quite different. The Nicaraguans have named this the "Güegüence effect," reflecting a close identification with the character.

The Güegüence effect has also come to mean other things. When Alemán was mayor of Managua, he erected statues of historical scenes at one of Managua's traffic circles and named it Güegüence Circle. The statues showed indigenous people trading with Europeans to honor Nicaragua's mestizo heritage. As president, Alemán and his top officials stole millions from the government. The figure of Güegüence appeared in the news many times. Alemán himself has been likened to the trickster. An apathetic attitude toward corruption seemed to seep into the national consciousness. If we are all Güegüence, then corruption is the logical outcome.

Some reject the idea of corruption at the center of the Nicaraguan national character. As one columnist wrote after the particularly dirty 2000 mayoral election:

> It seemed that the logic of the campaign is frightfully demonstrative of the way that in this "little country we are all corrupt" or "nobody is free of sin here, therefore nobody can throw the first stone." A sad drama for a country that has suffered so much.[23]

Even the Güegüence scholar Carlos Mántica shook his head vehemently at the idea that the character was the archetypal Nicaraguan. Why would anyone want to identify with a thief, a liar, and a child molestor?[24] To him, Güegüence was the tool of the colonial government as much as he subverted the government's power.

In a conversation with Zoa Mesa and Gonzalo Cuellar of Guachipilín, a children's puppet theatre, I asked if they thought Güegüence was the typical Nicaraguan. The group performed a play based on the character in 1989. Cuellar also rejected that idea, saying that the marriage at the end represents a marriage of political and economic power, both of which are equally corrupt. What interested Cuellar were the *machos,* or the black mules, who carry the Spanish and mestizo men who are "drunk with power." The mule characters are always present, always watching, but silent: "They are the only ones who really see what is happening."[25] Cuellar suggests that these are the indigenous people, who are often rendered invisible in the discourse of mestizo Nicaraguan politics.

The field for debate over the merits and faults of the Güegüence character opens ever wider as citizens employ the figure to define the nature of the Nicaraguan character. The contested figure arises out of Nicaragua's colonial past to stand in for either corruption or resistance, depending on the narrative. With the UNESCO decision, the Nicaraguans hope to fix the trickster, and the dance will be officially memorialized as a national performance.

Conclusion
Imaginings, Dreams, and Memories

The nationalist playwrights of Guatemala and Nicaragua have attempted to capture the nature of the nation and to stage it for the affirmation of their fellow citizens. They have tried to define, at that moment, the people, the culture, the boundaries, and the history of the nation. The plays have employed many of the same strategies to create a lasting portrait of a changing and dynamic phenomenon. In the ritual of imagining a nation, the dramatists have left little sites of a nation memorialized.

The nation as imagined community, or as memorialized in sites for memory (Nora's "lieux de mémoire"), leads to the next question for the Latin American nation poised on the verge of composing itself. Perhaps in the past the nation has come into being through the imaginings of the likes of Cuadra and the Vanguardia, whose call for a fascist dictator heralded the dynasty of Somoza, like Rolando Steiner's protagonist in *Judit*, who imagines a woman and finds he cannot destroy the imaginary world he has created. His self-destruction parallels the suicide of a nation of people who longed so much for stability within the volatile dynamics of Nicaraguan politics that they invited in a foreign power and a created a monster. Perhaps the nation has only existed in dreams, like the indigenous dreams of the family in Asturias's *Soluna* that form part of a search for the appropriated Guatemalan culture. But the imagined community of the nation relies upon its cultural memory to balance its aspirations. The community must see itself "moving steadily down (or up) history."[1]

Because nationalist writers seek to memorialize the nation and the national history through its dramatization, it may be true that they participate in the imperialist discourse of forgetting, part of the cycle of patricide that writers such as Cuadra fear. Gómez-Peña performs forgetting and remembering in *1992*:

Remember me?
I used to be . . . I used to be . . . I used to be . . .
I looked so pitiful
that I decided to hide in my memory. . . .
I became an immigrant
the day I was forbidden to remember.
los españoles no nos permitieron recordar.
the French didn't allow us to remember.
the Americans still don't want us to remember.[2]

In memory lies the power of ownership of identity. The power is taken away if the memory is forbidden or questioned. This is what Gómez-Peña means when he refers to the "estado de coma global" (state of global coma).[3] Everyone is made to forget, because classification in the world order is assigned by hegemonic relationships. Gómez-Peña says:

wait, my memory is failing again
are you the cousin of the uncle
of the mother of someone
I can't remember?
or am I making it up
'cause after all
this is just a bad performance
in a country that has forbidden memory?
a country whose name I can't even remember
USA I think United States of Am . . . nesia
. . . .
wait, my memory is coming back.[4]

Perhaps the next step is to remember, to refuse in some way to participate in the project of erasure and forgetting that is in some way imposed by larger economic powers at the center.

This "syntax of forgetting," as Bhabha calls it, resides at the basis of nation formation.[5] To unify the diverse contingencies of Nicaragua, Violeta Chamorro found it necessary to erase, to forget. Chamorro is the widow of Pedro Joaquín Chamorro, the newspaper editor of *La Prensa,* the opposition newspaper before and after the revolution. As part of her candidacy, Violeta Chamorro emphasized that she would act in her husband's place, the brave martyr who died for his nation fighting for the revolution. In a parade before the election, Violeta Chamorro rode on a float in a wheelchair, symbolizing her desire to "heal" the nation. Part of this healing involved painting over murals, erasing, and forgetting the memory by wiping clean the sites of memory.

Groups such as Ocho de Marzo are part of the project of remembering. For the women who participate in the local site of community and nation building, the site is one of lived memory (Nora's "milieux de mémoire"). The site displays the difference of individual memory, where the women recognize one another but do not seek identification. The national culture lives in rupture, in memory, and in true healing.

The statue fragment of the dictator Somoza was last suspended in a vortex of signification. It rested in the plaza of the Palacio Nacional as part of the Sandinista project of redefining the legacy of Somoza. It was painted into the mural *Our Land Is Made of Courage and Glory,* which recounts the long journey of Nicaraguan history. The last time I visited Managua, in 2002, my friend took me to La Loma de Tiscapa, the former Somoza military base and the theatre of the last hours of Sandino's life. In 1990 the Sandinistas erected a huge, steel silhouette of Sandino, which can be seen from much of the city of Managua. There, at the base of the structure, was the rear of the horse. It had been removed from the plaza and placed at the feet of the hero. The Nicaraguans saw fit to memorialize the fragment, removing it from the daily discourse of the National Plaza and laying it to rest, at least for now, in a site of memory. In the theatre of national history, the dictator has been vanquished by the legacy of Sandino, the assassin conquered by his victim.

The national theatre and its drama, the deployment of national metaphors, and the ordering of the nation's history have made up the projects of the playwrights I have discussed. They have achieved varying degrees of success in soliciting agreement from the citizens in the audience and in establishing theatrical traditions. But the performance of the nation has reached a crisis as the postcolonial nations are expressed across national borders through either transnational solidarity or migration or exile. For this reason, the process of nation building may occur less under the metanarrative of the proscenium arch in the national theatre and more in the local sites and the interstices between borders.

NOTES
BIBLIOGRAPHY
INDEX

Notes

Introduction

1. Villegas, 506.
2. McMurray, 272.
3. Dreyer, 186.
4. Anderson, 5.
5. Cohen, 36.
6. Lowenthal, 38.
7. Gellner, 57.
8. Bolt, *Banana Republic*, 11. Alan Bolt often publishes under the name Allan Bolt. Throughout this book, all translations from the Spanish are mine unless otherwise noted in the bibliography.
9. Mary Karen Dahl used the term *institutionally privileged* in "Postcolonial British Theatre," 40.

1. Historical Background

1. Brinton, viii.
2. http://www.pcusa.org/pcusa/wmd/ep/country/guademo.htm.
3. Brinton, xi.
4. http://www.pcusa.org/pcusa/wmd/ep/country/nicdemo.htm.
5. Grube, 201–18.
6. Brinton, xxiv.
7. For a detailed description of indigenous performance typologies, see Judith Weiss et al. *Latin American Popular Theatre*, 27–33.
8. Brinton, xxiii.
9. Carrillo, 41.
10. Weiss et al., 29.
11. Versényi, 33.
12. Walter, 3–4.
13. Pianca, *El teatro de nuestra América*, 15.
14. Gellner, 25.
15. Diamond and Linz, 5.
16. Pianca, 15.

17. Solórzano, 12.
18. Ibid., 1–2.
19. Ibid., 73.

2. Nationalism and the Performance of the Nation

1. Diriangén was a sixteenth-century indigenous leader of a well-planned attack against Spanish troops.
2. The pronoun for *you* in this case is *sos*, a Castilian informal form reserved only for those who are very dear and familiar to the speaker. The pronoun is used in some Latin American countries.
3. Anderson, 482.
4. Brennen, 63.
5. Galeano, 13.
6. Gellner, 7.
7. Anderson, 24.
8. Ibid., 26.
9. Ibid., 62–63.
10. Gellner, 154.
11. Fanon, 35.
12. Sommer, 39.
13. Fernández Retamar, 27.
14. Anderson, 5.
15. Hobsbawm, 7.
16. Kruger, *The National Stage*, 3.
17. Taylor, *Disappearing Acts*, 29.
18. Butler, 18.
19. Terdiman, 17.
20. Taylor, 30.
21. Bhabha, *Nation and Narration*, 3.

3. Guatemalan National Theatre

1. Carrillo, 45.
2. Allen, 274.
3. Ibid.

4. Carrillo, 45.

5. Allen, 274.

6. Solórzano, 34.

7. Ibid., 35.

8. Carrillo, 46.

9. James, 55.

10. Ibid., 57.

11. Shillington, 48.

12. Bennett, 101.

4. Manuel Galich and *Mestizaje*

1. Balibar, 54.

2. Underiner, 14–58.

3. Robleto, 47.

4. Ibid., 241.

5. Galich, *La mugre,* 355.

6. Ibid., 380.

7. Galich, *El pescado indigesto,* 93.

8. Ibid.

9. McMurray, 273.

10. Galich, *El tren amarillo,* 40.

11. Ibid., 33.

12. Ibid., 42.

13. Ibid., 30.

14. Ibid., 39.

15. Ibid., 75.

16. Ibid., 60.

17. Galich uses the word *suampo,* which appears in his glossary as a uniquely Guatemalan term. Although the word phonetically matches the English *swamp,* the more common word for *swamp* is *pantano,* 44.

18. Ibid., 45.

5. European Thought and Indigenous Dreams

1. Bolt, *Banana Republic,* 31.

2. Sandino, 87.

3. Pablo Antonio Cuadra, *Por los caminos van los campesinos,* 16.

4. Ibid.

5. Randy Martin, *Socialist Ensembles,* 106.

6. Steven F. White, 33.

7. Martin, *Socialist Ensembles,* 106.

8. Fernández Morales, 78.

9. Ibid., 82.

10. Ibid., 82.

11. Ibid., 82.

12. *Zambo* refers to people of indigenous and African descent.

13. Fernández Morales, 84.

14. Galeano, 39.

15. McMurray, 272–73.

16. McMurray, 21.

17. Camayd-Freixas, 207–25.

18. Asturias, "Magia y política," quoted in Erik Camayd-Freixas, 209.

19. Asturias, *Men of Maize,* 163–64.

20. Gerald Martin, xiii.

21. Asturius, *Soluna,* 14.

22. Ibid., 15.

23. Ibid., 22–23.

24. Ibid., 26–27.

25. Ibid., 30–31.

26. Ibid., 39–40.

27. Ibid., 45.

28. Ibid., 47–49.

29. Ibid., 49.

30. Ibid., 64–65.

31. Ibid., 75–76.

32. Camayd-Freixas, 208.

33. Camayd-Freixas, 208, and Hurtado Heras.

34. Gerald Martin, xiii.

35. Hurtado Heras.

36. Morales, 419.

37. Ibid., 420.

6. Nicaraguan National Theatre

1. Layera, 1035.

2. Walter, 9.

3. Ibid., 15.

4. O'Quinn-Havens, 82–83.

5. Walter, 15–16.

6. Selser, 70.

7. Ibid., 152.

8. Walter, 31.

9. O'Quinn-Havens, 51–57.

10. Ibid., 53.

11. Solórzano, 81.

12. Bolt, interview by author, February 1989.

13. Renan, 19.

14. Roberts, 3.

15. Ibid., 4.

16. Ibid., 196–97.

17. Mason, 2.

18. Ibid., 10.

19. Deane, 10.

20. Ibid., 9.

21. Lowenthal, 40.

22. Ibid., 44.

23. Ibid., 44.

7. Alan Bolt and Identification with the Struggle in *Banana Republic*

1. Versényi, 124.

2. Bolt, "El teatro estudiantil universitario," 5.

3. Ibid., 8.

4. Versényi, 165.

5. Bolt, "El teatro estudiantil universitario," 12.

6. O'Quinn-Havens, 70.

7. Randy Martin, 98.

8. Versényi, 166.

9. Bolt states this in "Para nosotros, teatristas, la revolucion es teatro," when he says, "Our theatre is born of that collective essence although there is a playwright, because I do the writing, but my works are not mine alone." 45 (Havana: Casa de las Americas, 1980), 82.

10. This is according to Kaiser-Lenoir, 126.

11. Ibid.

12. Bolt, *Banana Republic*, 12.

13. Ibid., 13.

14. Ibid., 14.

15. Ibid., 21.

16. Ibid., 24.

17. Ibid., 32.

18. Ibid., 40.

19. Based on a personal interview with Alan Bolt, La Praga, February 1989.

20. Asturias, 78.

21. Lowenthal, 53.

22. Ibid., 57.

23. Ibid., 61–62.

24. Ibid., 63.

25. Many of the writings of Karl Marx develop his ideas on historical materialism, from *The German Ideology* to the *Manifesto of the Communist Party*.

26. For an analysis of Freud's concept of aggression and the Oedipal impulse in society, see *Civilization and Its Discontents*.

27. Marx, 473–74.

8. Pablo Antonio Cuadra and the Crimes of the Brother Clan

1. Marcuse, 89–90.

2. Ibid., 91.

3. Cuadra, *Canciones de pájaro y señora (Songs of the Bird and the Lady)*, originally published in 1935. Available at http://www.dariana.com/Panorama/PAC-poemas.htm#anchor591672.

4. Ibid.

5. Cuadra, *Por los caminos van los campesinos*, 17.

6. Ibid., 18.

7. Ibid., 19.

8. Ibid., 22.

9. Ibid., 27.

10. Ibid., 50.

11. Ibid., 55.

12. Ibid.

13. Ibid., 62–63.

14. Ibid., 90.

15. Layera, 1038.

16. Ibid.
17. Cuadra, 100–101.
18. Ibid., 101.
19. Ibid., 102.
20. Layera, 1038–39.
21. Ibid., 1038.
22. Taylor, "Framing the Revolution," 84.
23. Ibid., 89–90.
24. Martin, *Socialist Ensembles,* 100.

9. Rolando Steiner and the Invention of Tradition
1. Hobsbawm, 1.
2. Ibid., 2.
3. Ibid., 9.
4. Layera, 1035.
5. Solórzano, 59.
6. Unruh, 37.
7. Cuadra, 14.
8. Layera, 1036.
9. Solórzano, 58.
10. Layera, 1035–36.
11. Cuadra, "Primer Manifesto," 26, as cited in O'Quinn-Havens, 35.
12. Bolt, *Banana Republic,* 11.
13. Terdiman, 21.
14. Nora, 7.
15. Ibid.
16. Rubin and Solórzano, 339.
17. Steiner, 64.
18. Ibid.
19. Ibid., 67.
20. Ibid., 69.
21. Ibid., 70.
22. Ibid.
23. Ibid., 71.
24. Abelardo Cuadra, 7. Abelardo Cuadra was a soldier present at the initial planning of the attack.

10. Interweavings, Hybrid Identities, and Contested Narratives
1. Bhabha, *Location of Culture,* 2.
2. Ibid., 9.

3. Randy Martin, xxvi.
4. Fanon, 225.
5. Kruger, "'That Fluctuating Movement of National Consciousness,'" 159.
6. Enloe, 161.
7. Ocho de Marzo program, March 1994.
8. Foucault, 93.
9. Ibid., 101.
10. Andersen, 61.
11. Ibid., 53.
12. Chatterjee, 81.
13. Bhabha, *Nation and Narration,* 6.
14. Gomez-Peña, 20.
15. Fanon, 225.
16. Olaniyan, 488–89.
17. Fernández Retamar, 14.
18. Bhabha, *Location of Culture,* 231.
19. Ibid., 231.
20. Ruíz Baldelomar.
21. Juárez Polanco.
22. "Happy Birthday, Señor Fox."
23. García Castillo.
24. Based on a personal interview, Managua, 15 October 2002.
25. Cuellar, personal interview, Managua, 17 October 2002.

Conclusion: Imaginings, Dreams, and Memories
1. Anderson, 26.
2. Gómez-Peña, 95, 103–4.
3. Ibid., 109.
4. Ibid., 133.
5. Bhabha, *Location of Culture,* 160.

Bibliography

Aguilar, Luis E. *Cuba 1933: Prologue to Revolution*. London: Cornell University Press, 1972.

Albuquerque, Severino. *Violent Acts: A Study of Contemporary Latin American Theatre*. Detroit: Wayne State University Press, 1991.

Allen, Richard F. *Teatro hispanoamericano: Una bibliografía anotada*. Boston: G. K. Hall, 1987.

Andersen, Julie K. Hay que ser muy mujer/To Be Very Much a Woman: Nicaraguan Women Confront Domestic Violence. Masters thesis, University of Iowa, 1994.

Anderson, Benedict R. O'G. *Imagined Communities: Reflections on the Origin and Spread of Nationalism*. London: Verso, 1983.

Arce, Manuel José. "Viva Sandino! Sandino debe nacer." *Alero* 3.13 (1975): 25–61.

Asturias, Miguel Ángel. *La audiencia de los confines*. Buenos Aires: Ariadna, 1957.

———. "Magia y política," *Indice* 226 (1967): 38–41. Quoted in Camayd-Freixas.

———. *Men of Maize*. Translated by Gerald Martin. Pittsburgh: University of Pittsburgh Press, 1984.

———. *Soluna*. Buenos Aires: Editorial Losange, 1955.

Babrusinkas, Julio. "Prólogo." In Galich, *El tren amarillo*, 5–22.

Balibar, Etienne. "Racism and Nationalism." In *Race, Nation, Class: Ambiguous Identities*, edited by Etienne Balibar and Immanuel Wallerstein, translated by Chris Turner, 37–67. London: Verso, 1988.

Bennett, Susan. *Theatre Audiences: A Theory of Production and Reception*. London: Routledge, 1990.

Bhabha, Homi K., ed. *The Location of Culture*. New York: Routledge, 1994.

———. *Nation and Narration*. New York: Routledge, 1993.

Bolt, Alan. "Banana Republic." *Cuadernos universitarios* 28 (1982): 9–40.

———. "Para nosotros, teatristas, la revolucion es teatro." *Conjunto* 45 (1980): 81–84.

———. Personal interview by author. La Praga, February 1989.

———. "El teatro estudiantil universitario: notas de Alan Bolt." *Conjunto* 45 (1980): 5–13.

Bravo-Elizondo, Pedro. "Manuel Galich (1913–1984)." *Latin America Theatre Review* 18.1 (1984): 4.

Brennan, Timothy. "The National Longing for Form." In Bhabba, *Nation and Narration*, 44–70.

Brentlinger, John. "Nicaragua and the Politics of Representation." *Confluencia* 6.1 (1990): 3–15.

Brinton, Daniel, ed. and trans. *The Güegüence; A Comedy Ballet in the Nahuatl-Spanish Dialect of Nicaragua*. Philadelphia: D. G. Brinton, 1883. Library of Aboriginal American Literature, no. 3. Reprint, New York: AMS Press, 1969.

Butler, Judith. "Imitation and Gender Insubordination." In *Inside/Out: Lesbian Theories, Gay Theories,* edited by Diana Fuss, 13–31. New York: Routledge, 1991.

Camayd-Freixas, Erik. "Miguel Ángel Asturias, *Hombres de maíz:* como lectura surrealista de la escritura mayense." *Revisita de critica literaria latinoamericana* 24.47 (1998): 207–25.

Carrillo, Hugo. "Orígenes y desarrollo del teatro guatemalteco." *Latin America Theatre Review* 5.1 (1971): 39–48.

Chatterjee, Partha. *Nationalist Thought in the Colonial World: A Derivative Discourse?* London: Zed Books for the United Nations, 1986.

Cohen, Isaac. "A New Latin American and Caribbean Nationalism." *The Annals of the American Academy of Political and Social Science,* 526 (March 1993): 36–46.

Collinson, Helen, and Lucinda Broadbent, eds. *Women and Revolution in Nicaragua.* London: Zed Books, 1990.

Cuadra, Abelardo. *Bohemia* (Havana) (13 Feb. 1949): 7.

Cuadra, Pablo Antonio. *Por los caminos van los campesinos.* San Jose, Costa Rica: Libro Libre, 1986.

Cuellar, Gonzalo. Personal interview. Managua, 17 October 2002.

Dahl, Mary Karen. "Postcolonial British Theatre: Black Voices at the Center." In *Imperialism and Drama: Essays on World Theatre, Drama and Performance,* edited by J. Ellen Gainor, 38–55. London: Routledge, 1995.

Deane, Seamus. Introduction to *Nationalism, Colonialism, and Literature,* edited by Fredric Jameson, Edward W. Said, and Terrence Eagleton, 3–19. Minneapolis: University of Minnesota Press, 1990.

Diamond, Larry, and Juan J. Linz, eds. *Democracy in Developing Countries.* Boulder, CO: L. Rienner, 1988.

Dolan, Jane Maureen. "The SelfEmpowerment of Women in Nicaragua: The Process of 'Collective Remembering.'" Ph.D. diss., University of Wisconsin–Madison, 1988.

Dreyer, Kevin. "Hugo Carrillo: 1928–1994." *Latin American Theatre Review* 28.1 (Fall 1994): 185–86.

Enloe, Cynthia. *Does Khaki Become You?* Boston: South End, 1983.

Estrada, Fatima. Personal interview by author. Managua, February 1989.

Fanon, Frantz. *The Wretched of the Earth.* Translated by Constance Farrington. New York: Grove, 1963.

Fernández Morales, Enrique. "La Niña del río." *Boletín nicaragüense de bibliografía y documentación* 41 (1943): 75–86.

Fernández Retamar, Roberto. *Caliban and Other Essays.* Translated by Edward Baker. Minneapolis: University of Minnesota Press, 1989.

Foucault, Michel. *The History of Sexuality.* Translated by Robert Hurley. New York: Vintage, 1978.

Freud, Sigmund. *Civilization and Its Discontents.* Translated by Joan Riviere. London: Hogarth, 1930.

Frundt, Henry J. "Guatemala in Search of Democracy." *Journal of Interamerican Studies and World Affairs* 32 (1990): 42–56.

Gainor, J. Ellen, ed. *Imperialism and Theatre*. New York: Routledge, 1995.

Galeano, Eduardo. *Guatemala: Occupied Country*. Translated by Cedric Belfrage. New York: Monthly Review Press, 1967.

Galich, Manuel. "M'hijo el bachiller." *Obras de teatro*. Vol 1. Guatemala: Editorial de ministerio de educación pública, 1943.

———. *El tren amarillo*. Havana: Editorial Letras Cubanas, 1979.

García Castillo, Carlos. "La recta final." *Boletín informativo de Nicaragua* 40. Fundación Popol Na. http://users.libero.it/itanica/popol_na/anno2000/pn37_da_15_a_21_ott_2000/ boletin.rtf.

Gellner, Ernest. *Nations and Nationalism*. New York: Cornell University Press, 1983.

Gilbert, Helen. *Sightlines: Race, Gender, and Nation in Contemporary Australian Theatre*. Ann Arbor: University of Michigan Press, 1998.

Gómez-Peña, Guillermo. *Walks on Water*. Edited by Deborah Levy. London: Methuen Drama, 1992.

Greenblatt, Stephen J. *Learning to Curse: Essays in Early Modern Culture*. New York: Routledge, 1990.

Grube, Nikolai. "Classic Maya Dance: Evidence from Hieroglyphs and Iconography." *Ancient Mesoamerica* 3.2 (1992): 201–18.

"Happy Birthday, Señor Fox." *Economist*. 7 February 2004, http://www.economist.com/displaystory.cfm?story_id=4557.

Harris, Max. *The Dialogical Theatre: Dramatizations of the Conquest of Mexico and the Question of the Other*. New York: St. Martin's Press, 1993.

Hobsbawm, Eric. *The Invention of Tradition*. Cambridge: Cambridge University Press, 1983.

Hoge, Warren. "Nicaraguan Women: Equals in Battle, Not in Home." *New York Times*, 11 January 1982, sec. B, p. 8.

Hurtado Heras, Saúl. "La biografía no escrita de Asturias," *Jornada Semanal* Suplemento Cultural 306, Benito Juárez, México, 1 January 2001. http://www.jornada.unam.mx/2001/ene01/010114/sem-hurtado.html.

James, Daniel. *Red Design for the Americas: Guatemalan Prelude*. New York: Day, 1954.

Jonas, Suzanne, and Nancy Stein. "The Construction of Democracy in Nicaragua." *Latin American Perspectives* 17.3 (1990): 10–37.

Jones, Willis Knapp. *Breve historia del teatro latinoamericano*. Mexico City: Ediciones de Andrea, 1956.

Juárez Polanco, Ulises. "Cuál es el Güegüence que corre en nuestra sangre." *El Nuevo Diario* (Managua). 1 February 2004, http://www-ni.elnuevodiario.com.ni/archivo/2004/febrero/01-febrero-2004/opinion/opinion2.html (accessed 14 March 2004).

Kaiser-Lenoir, Claudia. "Nicaragua: Theatre in a New Society." *Theatre Research International* 14.2 (1989): 122–30.

Kovacci, Ofelia. "Una muestra del teatro popular en Nicaragua: *El Güegüence.*" *Filologia* 21.2 (1986): 179–99.

Kruger, Loren. *The National Stage.* Chicago: University of Chicago Press, 1992.

———. "'That Fluctuating Movement of National Consciousness': Protest, Publicity, and Postcolonial Theatre in South Africa." In *Imperialism and Theatre: Essays on World Theatre, Drama and Performance,* 148–63. London: Routledge, 1995.

Lakoff, George, and Mark Johnson. *Metaphors We Live By.* Chicago: University of Chicago Press, 1980.

Layera, Ramón. "De la vanguardia al teatro nicaraguense actual: valoración de Pablo Antonio Cuadra." *Revista iberoamericana* 57.157 (1991): 1033–41.

Lindenberger, Herbert Samuel. *Historical Drama: The Relation of Literature and Reality.* Chicago: University of Chicago Press, 1975.

Lowenthal, David. *The Past Is a Foreign Country.* Cambridge: Cambridge University Press, 1985.

Lukacs, Gyorgy. *The Historical Novel.* Translated by Hannah Mitchell and Stanley Mitchell. London: Merlin Press, 1962.

Mac Dougall, Jill R. *Performing Identities on the Stages of Quebec.* New York: Peter Lang, 1997.

Mántica Abaunza, Carlos. *El cuecuence o el gran sinvergüenza.* Managua: Academia Nicaragüense de la Lengua, 2001.

———. Personal interview by the author. Managua, 15 October 2002.

Marceles Daconte, Eduardo. "Manuel Galich: La identidad del teatro latino-americano." *Latin America Theatre Review* 17.2 (1984): 55–63.

Marcuse, Herbert. *Eros and Civilization.* Boston: Beacon Press, 1955.

Martin, Gerald. Introduction to *Men of Maize,* by Miguel <Aa>ngel Asturias, translated by Gerald Martin, xi–xxxii. Pittsburgh: University of Pittsburgh Press, 1984.

Martin, Randy. *Socialist Ensembles: Theater and State in Cuba and Nicaragua.* Minneapolis: University of Minnesota Press, 1994.

———. "Theater After the Revolution: Refiguring the Political in Cuba and Nicaragua." In *On Edge: The Crisis of Contemporary Latin American Culture,* edited by George Yudice, Jean Franco, and Juan Flores, 115–40. Minneapolis: University of Minnesota Press, 1992.

Marx, Karl. "The Manifesto of the Communist Party." In *The Marx-Engels Reader,* edited by Robert C. Tucker, 469–500. New York: W. W. Norton, 1978.

Mason, Jeffrey D. *Melodrama and the Myth of America.* Bloomington: Indiana University Press, 1993.

McMurray, George R. *Spanish American Writing Since 1941: A Critical Survey.* New York: Ungar, 1987.

Mira, Joan F. "On Speaking and Being: Identity, Language, Nation," translated by Sean Golden. *Catalonia Review,* 1 December 1987: 8496.

Montes Huidobro, Matias. "Teatro en Lunes de Revolución." *Latin America Theatre Review* 18.1 (1984): 17–34.

Morales, Mario Roberto. "Aldea oral/ciudad letrada: La apropiación vanguardista de lo popular en América Latina: El caso de Miguel Ángel Asturias y las *Leyendas de Guatemala.*" *Revista Iberoamericana* 62.175 (1996): 405–20.

Morton, Carlos. "The Nicaraguan Drama: Theatre of Testimony." *Latin America Theatre Review* 17.2 (1984): 89–92.

Murguialday, Clara. *Nicaragua, revolución y feminismo (1977–1989).* Madrid: Editorial Revolución, 1990.

Ngũgĩ wa Thiong'o. *Writers in Politics: Essays.* London: Heinemann Educational, 1981.

"Nicaragua—Performance After the Triumph: Two Views." *Drama Review* 31.4 (1987): 58–90.

Nora, Pierre. "Between Memory and History: Les Lieux de Mémoire," translated by Marc Roudebush. *Representations* 26 (1989): 7–25.

Ocho de Marzo. *Domestic Violence Scenario.* Directed by Fatima Estrada. Managua, Nicaragua, August 1989.

———. *Three Scenarios.* Play by Rosa Estela Valle Chavarria. Directed by Reyna Carmen Gomez Hurtado. Wisconsin Coordinating Council on Nicaragua. University of Wisconsin Memorial Union, Madison, Wisconsin, March 1993.

Olaniyan, Tejumola. "Dramatizing Postcoloniality: Wole Soyinka and Derek Wolcott." *Theatre Journal* 44.4 (1992): 485–500.

O'Quinn-Havens, Kathleen. "Politics and the National Theatre of Nicaragua." Ph.D. diss., University of South Carolina, 1989.

Pereira, Teresinha Alves. "La estructura de *El ultimo cargo.*" *Latin America Theatre Review* 8.1 (1974): 91–92.

Pianca, Marina. "Postcolonial Discourse in Latin American Theatre." *Theatre Journal* 41.4 (1989): 515–23.

———. *El teatro de nuestra América: un proyecto continental, 1959–1989.* Minneapolis: Institute for the Study of Ideologies and Literature, 1990.

Ray, Stan. "Language and Nation." *Linguist* 33.5 (1994): 170–71, 175.

Reiss, Timothy J. "Mapping Identities: Literature, Nationalism, Colonialism." *American Literary History* 4.4 (1992): 649–77.

Renan, Ernst. "What Is a Nation?" In *Nation and Narration,* edited by Homi K. Bhabha, translated by Martin Thom, 8–22. New York: Routledge, 1993.

Roberts, Spencer E. *Soviet Historical Drama: Its Role in the Development of a National Mythology.* The Hague: M. Nijhoff, 1965.

Robleto, Hernán. "Pájaros del norte." *Boletín nicaragüense de bibliografía y documentación* 49 (1936): 42–63.

Rosenberger, J. "Nicaragua: Vanishing Sandinista Murals." *Art in America* 81.7 (1993): 27.

Rubin, Don, and Carlos Solórzano. *The World Encyclopedia of Contemporary Theatre: The Americas.* New York: Routledge, 2001.

Ruíz Baldelomar, Leslie. "¿Conoces al gran pícaro?" *La Prensa* (Managua). 5 October 2003. http://www-ni.laprensa.com.ni/archivo/2003/octubre/05/revista/revista-2003/005-03.html (accessed 14 March 2004).

Said, Edward W. *Culture and Imperialism.* New York: Knopf, 1993.

Sandino, Augusto. *El pensamiento vivo de Sandino.* Edited by Sergio Ramirez. San Jose, Costa Rica: Editorial Universitaria Centroamericana, 1974.

Schlesinger, Stephen, and Stephen Kinzer. *Bitter Fruit: The Untold Story of the American Coup in Guatemala.* New York: Anchor, 1983.

Selser, Gregorio. *Sandino.* Translated by Cedric Belfrage. New York: Monthly Review Press, 1981.

Serna Servín, Juan Antonio. "La mujer como paradigma del duelo silencioso en la identidad en *Soluna* de M. A. Asturias." Paper presented as part of the annual conference Tercer Congreso de Teatro Latinoamericano. Lawrence, KS, 3 April 1997.

Shillington, John. *Grappling with Atrocity: Guatemalan Theater in the 1990s.* Madison, NJ: Fairleigh Dickinson University Press, 2002.

Solórzano, Carlos. *Teatro latinoamericano del siglo XX.* Buenos Aires: Ediciones Nueva Visión, 1961.

Sommer, Doris. *Foundational Fictions: The National Romances of Latin America.* Berkeley: University of California Press, 1991.

Spivak, Gayatri Chakravorty. *In Other Worlds: Essays in Cultural Politics.* New York: Routledge, 1987.

Steiner, Rolando. "La noche de Wiwilí." *Boletín nicaragüense de bibliografía y documentación* 49 (1982): 64–72.

Taylor, Diana. *Disappearing Acts: Spectacles of Gender and Nationalism in Argentina's "Dirty War."* Durham: Duke University Press, 1997.

———. "Framing the Revolution: *La Noche de los asesinos* and *Ceremonial de guerra.*" *Latin American Theatre Review* 24.1 (1990): 81–92.

Terdiman, Richard. "Deconstructing Memory: On Representing the Past and Theorizing Culture in France Since the Revolution." *Diacritics* 15.4 (1985): 13–35.

Underiner, Tamara. "Cultures Enacted/Cultures in Action: Performance, Community and Gender in Mayan Mexico." Ph.D. diss., University of Washington, 1997.

Unruh, Vicky. "The *Chinfonía burguesa:* A Linguistic Manifesto of Nicaragua's Avant-Garde." *Latin America Theatre Review* 20.2 (1987): 37–48.

Versényi, Adam. *Theatre in Latin America: Religion, Politics, and Culture from Cortes to the 1980s.* Cambridge: Cambridge University Press, 1993.

Villegas, Juan. "Historicizing Latin American Theatre." *Theatre Journal* 41.4 (1989): 505–14.

Walter, Knut. *The Regime of Anastasio Somoza, 1936–1956.* Chapel Hill: University of North Carolina Press, 1993.

Weiss, Judith, et al. *Latin American Popular Theatre: The First Five Centuries.* Albuquerque: University of New Mexico Press, 1993.

Whisnant, David E. *Rascally Signs in Sacred Places: The Politics of Culture in Nicaragua.* Chapel Hill: University of North Carolina Press, 1995.

White, Hayden. *Metahistory: The Historical Imagination in Nineteenth-Century Europe*. Baltimore: Johns Hopkins University Press, 1973.

White, Steven F. *Culture and Politics in Nicaragua: Testimonies of Poets and Writers*. New York: Lumen Books, 1986.

Wikander, Matthew H. *The Play of Truth & State: Historical Drama from Shakespeare to Brecht*. Baltimore: Johns Hopkins University Press, 1986.

Wisconsin Coordinating Council on Nicaragua. *Program from Three Scenarios*. Ocho de Marzo Performance, University of Wisconsin Memorial Union, Madison, Wisconsin, March 1993.

Zalacaín, Daniel. "Los recursos dramaticos en *Soluna*." *Latin America Theatre Review* 14.2 (1981): 19–25.

Index

E. J. Westlake, an assistant professor in theatre studies at the University of Michigan, has taught theatre history and playwriting at Auburn and Bowling Green State universities and has published essays on Latin American theatre, community-based theatre, and public art.

Theater in the Americas

The goal of the series is to publish a wide range of scholarship on theater and performance, defining theater in its broadest terms and including subjects that encompass all of the Americas.

The series focuses on the performance and production of theater and theater artists and practitioners but welcomes studies of dramatic literature as well. Meant to be inclusive, the series invites studies of traditional, experimental, and ethnic forms of theater; celebrations, festivals, and rituals that perform culture; and acts of civil disobedience that are performative in nature. We publish studies of theater and performance activities of all cultural groups within the Americas, including biographies of individuals, histories of theater companies, studies of cultural traditions, and collections of plays.